A Woman

Lora Kay

Also by Lora Kay

'Darkness in the Light' short stories

ISBN: 978-1-917129-92-3
Hardback edition

Contents

*To my mother, who taught me
independence and resilience,
but most of all, the freedom
of a woman's mindset.*

A Woman

She was sweet and pure and naive. She was ambitious and intelligent and successful. She was abused, molested, beaten, raped; she was even murdered. She was a woman. Is it hard being a woman? To tell the truth, it doesn't seem so. Subtle and delicate in her beauty and tenderness, spreading light and warmth across to anyone in her presence because it's just natural for her to do so. Capable of creating, giving and sharing love, women are the gentle half of humankind. The one to be caressed with flowers and kissed with the most gentle lips. Behind every man, there is one strong woman to support him, as the famous quote says.

How could anyone want to see fear and tears in a pair of beautiful eyes that were born only to express joy? The honest answer comes baring a sobering reality, the reality of an illusion firmly refuted.

Toronto, Canada

Charlotte Anderson had turned eleven years old just a few days ago, and she already knew that her biggest birthday wish would not be coming true. It wasn't much she wanted, or at least, nothing that involved money, as was probably the case with most of the children her age. The only dream she had for the past three months was for her family to be whole again. Her father, William Anderson, left them because of his love affair with some 'slut', as her mother, Chloe, put it.

Charlotte didn't know much else about the woman who intruded into her family and took, robbed even, what wasn't hers to have, leaving broken pieces behind herself. As far as Charlotte understood, this unknown figure was like a mirage, imageless, with no tangible shape even in her mind; however, she had heard her mother's descriptions on a couple occasions – 'young', 'immoral', 'easy woman'. This was not essential, however.

The most disturbing part was that her home, which, until recently, was cosy, full of laughter and happiness, was now empty. Charlotte almost didn't want to go home after school because she knew she would find her mother crying, and the absence of her father was so severe that it was almost unbearable. Her heart was breaking from this new, unknown-until-now pain, from the loneliness and sadness she was feeling, from wanting so badly to be able to calm her mother, to tell her that everything was going to be alright – as her mother had done for her when she'd fallen and scraped her knee on the street. But these were unexplored pains for Charlotte; she didn't know if it would fade away as quickly as the one from the wound.

And as if all this wasn't already enough, the problems kept pouring. For the first time, Charlotte began to understand the importance of money. Chloe was now a single mother, and the funds were never enough – one more reason for the secret moments of collapse she would allow herself in the absence of her daughter. All the same, Charlotte always recognised when her mother had been crying. 'Nothing ever remains hidden' was Chloe's wise advice to her daughter, which could be effectively applied in many cases.

One Saturday morning, Charlotte's grandmother, Olivia, came to visit. Chloe had to work, taking some extra hours in the tailoring factory, and she needed someone to take care of little Charlotte. The child was more than happy to see her granny, who was also always busy working. Add to this the fact that she lived about an hour away and the little girl didn't get to see her very often at all. But whenever possible, Olivia travelled the distance to take care of her favourite granddaughter for as long as she was able, which Charlotte appreciated, even if she did have to be alone for the last hour or so until her mother got back home from work sometimes.

'Mother, thank you once again for doing this. You know I wouldn't ask if it wasn't absolutely necessary, but all these bills waiting to be paid and ...' Chloe's voice broke one day before heading off, a weak groan revealing her sadness.

Charlotte, who was listening behind the half-opened kitchen door, could imagine the expression on her mother's face. She didn't like seeing her like this; it was making her so upset that she wanted to cry along with her. Charlotte stood there, waiting for the right moment to enter and say 'hello' to her granny. She didn't want to interrupt the conversation, and it always made her uncomfortable when the pitiful looks turned and fixed on her, the 'oh, poor child'. Or worse, they might start talking about her dad. 'He might not care about his wife, but at least for his own daughter ... The soulless monster.'

Charlotte knew her father had great guilt, and many things around this were still not clear to the little girl, but it was never pleasant to listen to discussions of the whole situation. The verbal attacks against him and the showing of pity towards her – it all hurt too much.

'My dear, I won't allow you to think that you're an inconvenience to me! I am your mother and I will always do whatever I can to help you,' Olivia said, interrupting her sobbing daughter with a soothing voice. 'For me, it's such a happiness to spend more time with my granddaughter, and yet such a sadness that I can't be of more use to you ...' The pause that followed felt heavy with some hidden meaning. Charlotte, who was still listening behind the door, had no clue what it could mean, but a moment later it all became clear, '... my offer is still valid, and I will be more than happy if you just agree.'

'Mother, please don't insist,' Chloe wiped her tears and made an effort to even her voice so it wouldn't sound too miserable. 'Your flat is too small for all of us, and all my memories are here ...' She took a deep breath to keep herself calm and prevent another wave of sadness from crushing her. 'Charlotte and I are managing for now; I won't give up!' she stated more firmly.

'I know, my darling. I know. You are strong, exactly as I taught you, but think of the child.' Olivia kept trying to convince her daughter.

'You raised me all alone,' Chloe reminded her. 'When my father left us, you did it by yourself with no help. I swore I wouldn't allow the same to happen to me, that I wouldn't have to go down the same path, but here I am – a single mother.' Listening to her mother's trembling voice, Charlotte could imagine the tears on her cheeks.

'The difference is that I had nobody to help me, but you do!' Charlotte heard her grandmother continue. 'If you're scared that you're walking down the path of your nightmares, at least remember that you're lucky enough to have me. To ask for help isn't shameful, my dear. Drop this stubbornness and promise me that the moment you feel at the limit of your strength, you will gather your luggage and that sweet girl of yours and come to me. Promise me!' insisted Olivia.

'I promise ...' Chloe replied, barely above a whisper.

'Come on now; off you go. You don't want to be late for work,' Olivia said, allowing more cheer to show in her voice now.

'Actually, today I'll be a little late. I hope you don't mind staying until seven tonight?' Chloe asked, sounding much calmer now – the mother-daughter talks always helped. Charlotte, still listening, was relieved by the good shift in her mother's mood but also curious as to what would be keeping her from coming home on time.

'Of course not, but doesn't the factory close early on Saturday?'

'Yes, yes, it does, but I … have sort of a "date",' Chloe laughed nervously.

Olivia clapped her hands joyfully and hurried to ask, 'With who? Why haven't you mentioned anything to me till now?'

'Don't rush with the happy ending mother; it's probably not anything serious. To be honest, I'm not sure if I'm ready yet, and having Charlotte ... I can't just introduce her to some unknown man.'

'She is still a child, but I'm sure she would be happy to see you smiling. Don't underestimate her,' Olivia said, a small smirk beginning to grow on her face once the serious sentiment was out of the way. 'Now tell me about this mysterious man.'

'He's just a colleague from work, a few years older than me, but he's funny, makes me smile, which is important for me these days. He's a good listener. Oh! I better go.' Chloe said, her eye suddenly catching the time.

Chloe opened the kitchen door to find her daughter standing there with wild, open eyes. For a brief moment, they just looked at each other; she couldn't be sure how much of the conversation the child had heard.

'Here she is, my favourite granddaughter!' Olivia said, swooping in. 'Come on, quickly to the table; the pancakes I brought for you aren't getting any warmer.' Olivia's loud voice was the perfect sobering jostle to bring the young girl and her mother back to the moment. It was easier for everyone just to pretend as if there was nothing going on, and so they did. Charlotte climbed on one of the chairs and, with her tongue out, she started impatiently opening the box her grandmother got for her. Her mother kissed her forehead, grabbed her purse, and in the next second she was already locking the front door.

Even though the taste of her favourite pancakes was enough to distract the little girl for the moment, an unpleasant feeling had already begun to settle in her chest. She didn't like the mention of this 'unknown man' who was making her mother smile.

'We're going to have a great time today, you'll see,' started Olivia while making herself a coffee. 'First, we're going to have a look at your homework, and later on we can enjoy some cartoons or drawing, whatever you like. Are the pancakes delicious?'

Charlotte just nodded along, because her mouth was too full. Her grandmother giggled happily and caressed her soft brown hair.

Chloe got home at the time she had promised and hurried to kiss her daughter. Olivia had to head off straight away to get started on the long journey back home, but at the front door, when the two women were alone and Charlotte was hypnotised by the cartoons on the television, they managed to exchange a few words.

'Well, how was the date?' the older of the two whispered excitedly.

'Fine, I guess,' Chloe sighed and blushed a little. 'Owen is really nice and completely understands my situation. He isn't worried about connecting with a woman who already has a child, and not many men are capable of doing such a thing. In fact, he says he loves children, so that puts me at ease a bit.'

'Does he have children on his own?'

'No. He hasn't been married either, but he said that having children had been a dream of his and that he feels ready for it.' Chloe paused suddenly and looked down at her shoes, even though they had no importance to her right now. Her thoughts were somewhere far away, and she wore the expression of someone about to make an important, potentially life-altering decision. 'Maybe it's time for me to carry on. I mean *he* did without even thinking twice – why shouldn't I? Why should I suffer when I could be with someone who supports me; it's tough to be a single parent.'

'I know darling. I know ... You have the right to be happy. You both deserve to be happy, especially after what you've been through. Plus, it's been long enough; you can make the next step.' The woman held tightly to her daughter's hand for a brief, silent moment before taking her purse and leaving.

Chloe wiped a tear just before it fell. She was sick and tired of having her face wet. She didn't want to taste the salty little drops anymore. 'It's time for some changes.' She stated it as a fact.

Charlotte was lying on the bed, holding close to her stuffed dolphin, which she loved very much. Her mother sat next to her, exhaustedly closed her eyes for a moment and lightly massaged her temples with her fingers. She was tired, and it was obvious. She pulled on a little blanket to cover both Charlotte and herself. The little girl smiled thankfully to her mother, but quickly read in her eyes that she had something to tell her. She looked on questioningly while Chloe searched for the right words.

'Sweetie, you know how much I love you and that I want us to be happy, right?'

Charlotte nodded, but something she didn't like was the feeling coming along with the conversation; it felt like one of those conversations that lead to bad news.

'I hope you know that I will never love anyone more than you, and nobody will take your place in my heart, but... it's time to start living again. Many amazing moments are expecting us from now on, I promise.' It was already feeling difficult to talk, yet she hadn't even reached the main topic. Chloe cleared her throat and pressed forward. It was like skydiving, courage was needed for the jump, the rest was easy. 'You know how your father has another woman beside him? Well, I need a man beside me, because life is easier for two.'

'We are two.' Charlotte frowned not understanding.

Her mother smiled and caressed her. 'Yes, but two adults are needed to take care of you. We are going to be ... a complete family again. I'll have more time to spend with you, and everything will be alright, you'll see.'

Charlotte saw her mother's soft smile, but she could also see how it didn't reach her eyes, which remained somewhat sad. She didn't want her mother to be sad. The conversation she had witnessed secretly this morning in front of the kitchen rushed back to her memory. Her mother had said that this man was making her smile, and her grandmother had said that she should understand all this because she would want her mother to be happy. And so it was.

'Fine,' the little girl said.

'What do you mean by that?' Chloe asked, sensing an odd indifference.

Charlotte shrugged; the whole thing didn't really bother her. 'I don't mind the man I heard you discussing with Grandma.'

Chloe's eyes got all watery again, but this time from happiness and relief. She cuddled next to her daughter in a sudden and emotional display of affection. 'You'll see, everything will be alright ...' she whispered again.

The following Saturday night, Chloe had another date with Owen. The difference this time was that he was officially invited for dinner at their house. Of course, the idea behind this was for him to be introduced to her daughter and for their bonding to finally begin. Chloe was nervously excited, somehow even more than when she'd first gone on a romantic date with him; this was far more important – Charlotte had to like him, feel comfortable around him. If ever this was to be at all possible, she had to accept him as a father. The hopes for this evening were big.

The doorbell rang. Chloe smoothened her hair one last time and winked at Charlotte who wore braids in her hair and a red dress that fell to the knees. The girl wasn't really excited, but she was prepared to put forward her best manners, as she was taught.

Chloe opened the door, and there stood Owen. In one hand, he held a bottle of wine, which he hurriedly passed to her, and in the other, a little gift bag.

Charlotte gave him an inspecting look as he exchanged a few words with her mother. He wasn't very tall, and he didn't seem too strong; Charlotte noticed that he was actually kind of skinny. He wore glasses, which Charlotte thought made him look old, older than most adults her mom's age anyway – he looked nothing like her father.

'And that is my Charlotte,' Chloe proudly announced, turning all the attention over to her daughter.

Owen came closer and kneeled in front of her. 'It is a pleasure to meet you, Charlotte.' He stretched a hand towards her for a handshake. 'Your name is as beautiful as you are. You look like a doll, a copy of your mother of course.' He turned his head towards Chloe to honour her;

she was glowing. His smile was stretched happily on his face, but the girl didn't like it, even though she couldn't say why.

'This is for you,' he continued, handing her the gift bag.

Charlotte took it with a shy smile and tried to peek inside without anyone noticing. Her mother had taught her to wait until she was alone to unpack her gifts; otherwise, it would show bad manners.

'She's not usually this shy. I'm sure she'll be feeling a bit more comfortable very soon, believe me,' said Chloe, showing her guest the way to the kitchen where the dinner was already waiting.

'Ah, they're charming at any age,' commented Owen as he followed her.

For a moment Charlotte was alone, but she knew she had to join the others in the kitchen soon. The time was enough, however, to check her gift – a Barbie doll and a chocolate bar. There could be no better gift for a girl, even though she was a bit over the age to play with dolls, and at school she had often seen children mock others for 'acting like babies'. Now it was more fashionable among her classmates to act like adults, and even though she wanted to fit in that circle, she was too shy. Plus, she still enjoyed sitting and playing with her toys.

Her mother had always warned her against following others for the sake of just following blindly, and that one should do what one feels like. She'd told Charlotte to protect the child inside herself instead of trying to grow up too early. Charlotte liked this advice, even though she didn't fully understand it yet.

She was trying to balance the situation at school; she didn't want to be one of those kids who were always laughed at. The small group of girls she was in was quiet. They didn't cause any trouble, and nobody really noticed them. They were neither 'popular' nor 'losers'; it was a bit of a neutral zone she happened to find herself in, and it made her feel comfortable.

She quickly put her gifts in her room and hurried to the kitchen where she was expected.

The evening passed, and it actually wasn't all that bad. Her mother was right, Owen turned out to be funny, even though he seemed more like a boring teacher at first. He even managed to make her laugh, which had made her mother melt with happiness. And so she kept laughing – she laughed the next time and the time after that ... Wasn't that the reason she was accepting this man in the first place?

Owen, already an official partner of her mother, would only visit them for Saturday dinners for the first month. Once they even went out all together to a cinema to watch a recently-popular animated movie. Chloe found his choice of movie extremely amusing given he was a grown man. Though she obviously knew why he'd chosen it; sitting in the theatre among all the children, watching Owen's genuine excitement, similar to that of her daughter's, warmed Chloe's heart immensely.

Very soon, the man, new to this little family circle, started visiting them more often, not only on Saturdays but during the week too. Sometimes he even stayed overnight. Charlotte found this a little weird. She didn't mind Owen in their lives, especially seeing as her mother hadn't cried for so long. Plus, she was enjoying the gifts. Owen was trying really hard to win her over, so every time he came over, he'd bring a little something for her, and like any child in this unique situation, she wasn't about to complain. But why did he need to sleep there?

Something was bothering her, and it was a bit confusing to think about. True, she was 'just a child' and didn't understand much of the grown-up world, but the fact that her father had disappeared like a ghost, as though he'd never existed, made her feel strange. Now this man was

11

taking his place so easily, with all the smiles and gifts. She feared that soon her father would be completely forgotten, and she still loved him …

It was Friday, the last day of the school week, and Charlotte had just experienced something completely new. During recess, while everybody played what they fancied most, one of the boys in her class was playfully chasing another boy, both running around and laughing. When they passed by her, she felt the hand of one of them lightly touch her buttocks. She turned around with a questioning look, but he just winked at her and carried on with his game. She could feel herself going red – she was sure she'd turned the same shade as her favourite dress. Zoey, one of her closest friends, giggled, having witnessed the whole thing.

'I think you have an admirer,' she joked.

Charlotte made a sound of disgust.

'Nathan is cute. He can be your boyfriend,' her friend continued.

'If you think he's cute, you be his girlfriend! I don't like anybody; the whole thing disgusts me,' Charlotte said fiercely, making her stance on the matter and her opinion of the joke quite clear.

'Having a boyfriend is cool!' Zoey tried to explain to her stubborn friend.

'And how do you know that?' Charlotte asked, feeling a little calmer now that her embarrassment was fading.

'Well, if you must know, once I had a boyfriend,' Zoey announced proudly.

'Really?' Charlotte was sceptical.

'Yes, but it was only for one day and we didn't even kiss,' the other girl explained, sounding a little disappointed.

They continued with the jokes and laughter till the end of the period. After that, the school day came to an end surprisingly quickly. When the final bell rang marking,

Charlotte was surprised to find out that it wasn't her mother who had come to pick her up. Instead, there was Owen. She walked slowly towards him, waiting there with his soft smile.

'Hi sweetie, I'm picking you up and bringing you home today,' he announced his responsible task.

'Where's my mom?' she asked. Even though her mom wasn't there, she didn't want to leave without her.

'Unfortunately, she got held at work for a couple of extra hours, so she asked me to take care of you until she came back. And I, of course, am happy to do it; you know how much I love spending time with you, right?' he winked at her, sounding excited, but this only made Charlotte freeze. It frightened her, but she wasn't sure why.

While she was looking at him blinking and not moving from her place, he gently put a hand on her shoulder and softly pushed her to the open door of the car.

The feeling of uncertainty panicked the little girl, and her hands struggled to fasten her seat belt. Owen's hand quickly came to the rescue of this little trouble. With ease, the belt made a click sound which, the sound of things successfully locking, but this unwanted help did nothing to make Charlotte any calmer. Cold sweat made her body shiver when she felt Owen's hand lightly slip on her thigh on its way back to the car wheel.

She didn't react. She didn't know how to. Did she understand if anything had happened at all, or if something had happened, she didn't know what it was. Her mind flashed back to what had happened during recess that day. A boy had intentionally touched her and then winked the same way Owen just did. Her friend Zoey said that this was a clear sign he liked her.

Charlotte felt sick.

It couldn't be. Her mother's boyfriend couldn't like her – he was an adult, and he was meant to be like a father to her! Charlotte didn't know what to think, but one thing was sure, she was already scared and wanted to see her mother.

The ride home wasn't long, but to her, every second spent with that man was an unpleasant stretch of the time. When they finally walked into the apartment, Owen said enthusiastically, 'You know, my little Charlotte, I do have another surprise for you, because you are such a good girl.' He smiled softly.

'When will my mother get back?' was the only question she asked – she wasn't interested in any gifts.

'Don't worry, she'll be here soon. Now, the plan is for us to watch a movie.'

'I have homework to do.' The girl was trying desperately to avoid any situation in which she had to stay with him.

'Of course, after the movie, we'll get to work on your school stuff, but I'm sure that, like every child, homework isn't your favourite part of the day. That's why I thought I'd give you some time off with a movie. It'll be our little secret; we don't want to upset your mother, right?' He winked at her again and invited her to sit on the couch.

She sat down, unable to feel comfortable, as she usually did as she was about to watch a movie. Something had her tense, even though the idea of postponing homework was appealing. She expected Owen to put a disk into the DVD player, but instead, he opened up his laptop. He got himself comfortable, right next to her. Charlotte didn't like how close he was, but she was already at the edge of the couch with nowhere else to move.

He pressed play, and Charlotte tried to understand the picture that had appeared on the screen. Something wasn't right – the movie was very strange. The woman on the screen had started taking her clothes off till she was completely naked. Charlotte couldn't believe she was seeing this; any time she watched a movie with her mom and her dad, if the actors even had to kiss, her father had always made her cover her eyes, saying that she was still a child and shouldn't be seeing stuff like that.

Shortly after, a man appeared on the screen that Charlotte was watching now – he too was completely naked. This shocked the little girl so much that she instinctively covered her eyes.

'Don't worry,' Owen said, 'it's nothing bad. Look, look, they seem to enjoy it.' Owen then forcibly took her little hands away from her eyes and placed them on her thighs, where he kept his hand together with hers.

Tears filled the little girl's eyes – she didn't like this man anymore. Whatever he was doing was wrong, and she was completely aware of it. His hand, which until now had been holding hers and keeping her from covering her eyes again, must have felt the lack of resistance and had finally relaxed. His fingers slid to the inside of her thigh, and the girl instinctively squeezed her legs. Why wasn't she able to move, to escape, to scream for help ... Why was she so paralysed and unable to command her body to get up and run away?

A ring from the home phone made them both jump. Owen removed his hand and Charlotte, now free, ran to get the call.

'Hello?' she said with a trembling voice.

'Charlotte, sweetheart, how are you?' It was her grandmother.

For Charlotte, in that moment, there was no greater relief than hearing her favourite granny's voice.

'I'm fine, just got back from school,' she answered, nervously taking a quick look at Owen, who had now closed the laptop and, with a calm smile, had pressed a finger to his lips, signalling to keep silent.

At this moment, the front door opened and Charlotte could hear the familiar voice of her mother. Owen rushed to her and embraced her in a loving hug. The child could see her mother's face, all glowing with happiness. Seeing her mother so happy, she remembered what her grandmother had said some time ago: 'She is still a child, but I'm sure she would be happy to see you smiling.' How could she break her mother's heart by admitting that the man she finally found, who was making her so happy, was doing something wrong to her daughter?

'Sweetie, are you still on the line?' The soft voice or her grandmother pulled her back.

'Yes, I'm sorry. I'm here, but mom just got home. We'll call you back later, okay?' The girl hung up, unable to continue a conversation; In fact, she was unable to do anything at all. She just wanted to close herself into her room.

'Darling, Owen's leaving. Do you want to come say goodbye, and maybe thank him for taking care of you?' her mother called from the hallway.

Charlotte didn't want to do any of that. Only for the sake of her mother did she show herself in the hallway, but she kept a visible distance. 'Bye,' she said, but she couldn't bring herself to be thankful.

'And ...' her mother coaxed, trying to bring out the manners that she'd taught her daughter, but there was only silence. 'I do apologise. I have no idea what's going on with her. Charlotte, what do you have to say to Owen?' she pressed a little more firmly.

'Thank you,' the girl said through a clenched jaw, but her mother seemed pleased, and Owen came and kneeled in front of her to give her a hug. He pressed his body into her and ever so subtly touched brushed his lips against her neck. Her mother didn't seem to be able to see.

'Don't worry Chloe, it was a pleasure to help. Plus, we really had fun together.'

'Thank you so much. I really appreciate it. It was all so unexpected, and there was nobody else to cover me at work, so I just had to stay,' she started justifying herself.

'I'm always here for whatever you need. I'll call you later.' He kissed her and left.

Chloe sighed, exhausted, and then remembered her daughter's behaviour.

'Young lady, to what do we owe the pleasure of your rude behaviour?' she asked a bit more sharply than she had intended.

Charlotte just looked at her, one long moment of eye contact. Two innocent child's eyes, frightened and hurt, were searching for something in their mother's eyes looking back but apparently, they didn't find what they were hoping for. Charlotte simply said, 'I have homework to do. I'm going back to my room.'

Chloe was standing there in the hallway, looking after her daughter with an open mouth, surprised. What was going on with this child, she wondered Was this the start of the early teenage stage?

The days passed, and Charlotte couldn't decide on if she should tell someone what had happened. She hadn't said a word until now, not even to her friends – especially not to them. She still wasn't fully sure what had happened exactly, but she knew it felt wrong. She didn't know if her friends would think she was weird or if they would get scared; they might even be scared of her. Or would they mock her? Considering Zoey's reaction after Nathan had playfully touched her, it was possible, but this all felt so different from what had happened with Nathan – the possible reactions scared her almost as much as the moment itself had.

It wasn't an option to talk to her mother either – she didn't want to hurt her. Maybe she would talk to her grandmother if it happened again at all. The truth was that the first person she wanted to talk to was her father. In her mind, he was strong, powerful, fearless, and protective of her. He didn't let anything bad happen to her, with the exception being that he wasn't around because he chose so. Plus, now three weeks had passed since the situation with nothing more happening, and she started wondering if maybe she had overreacted a little, maybe even imagined it.

That Friday night, Owen was going to come over for dinner, and he was going to be staying the night. 'Otherwise, it will be too late for him to leave,' as her mom had explained. Charlotte knew it was a lie. She was perfectly aware that her mom and dad used to do something in their room that only adults could do and that this was probably the same thing that her mom and Owen were going to do. This was apparently also how babies showed up, but she didn't care enough to know the details. On the contrary to her classmates and friends, she wasn't in a rush to grow up.

After dinner, Charlotte hurried back to her room, where she played with her toys until late because she didn't have to go to school the next day. When she looked at the clock, it was midnight already – she hadn't wanted to play until that late. Her mother would be angry if she found out, but she'd be even angrier if Charlotte didn't brush her teeth, so she decided to sneak off to the bathroom, quick and quiet. Owen and her mother should have already been asleep, but she didn't want to risk it and opted to tiptoe through the hallway. When she finally got to the bathroom, she noticed that the lights were on. However, she didn't hear any sound coming from behind the door, so she assumed someone must have left them on by accident – something she was definitely guilty of. She pushed the door open and walked in. In the next instant, she froze to the spot; standing there in front of her was Owen, having just gotten out of the shower. A white towel was wrapped around his waist, and his chest was bare. He smiled at her, welcomingly and friendly, and she felt the same cold shivers as the day on the couch. As if her muscles were made of jelly, she once again couldn't give them the order to move, to run away – she was paralysed by fear. Owen waved with his hand to invite her closer, but she didn't move. Then he made a big step towards her and pushed the door closed behind the child.

'Do you want me to show you something?' he asked kindly, like they were in a Luna Park and he was offering to buy her a treat. The towel he had around his waist suddenly fell to the floor, leaving him completely naked in front of the little girl.

Aside from that weird movie Owen had made her watch before, Charlotte had never seen a naked man, not even her father. Things again felt wrong. She wanted to call her mother for help. She was close, sleeping in the next room, but her throat was all dry.

'Do you want to touch it?' the man asked, keeping a friendly manner. He was acting as if all of this was normal, as if he were showing her his pet dog.

'No!' Charlotte's voice came back just enough for her to refuse.

'Come on, don't be shy. I'll show you how,' he insisted, reaching for her hand.

Charlotte shook her head in disagreement, but it wasn't enough to stop him. He took her hand and placed it on his intimate parts. The feeling was so disgusting. Hot tears started falling from the girl's eyes, and she tried to get away, but Owen seemed not to notice her effort – he had an odd expression on his face now. After maybe less than a minute, he finally let go of her hand. The man took his towel from the floor, and with one quick movement wrapped it back around himself to cover up. Once again he put a finger to his lips. 'Our little secret,' he said, and then he walked out of the bathroom.

Left alone, Charlotte hurried to the sink where she began washing her trembling hands. She rubbed the soap as hard as she could, until her hands became all red and even started hurting. She completely forgot to brush her teeth, even to dry her hands. All she wanted was to get out of the bathroom as soon as possible, scared that Owen might come back.

Charlotte ran to her room, no longer trying to keep quiet. She locked the door twice, and then, only then, when she finally felt safe behind the walls of her own room, did the child sit on the floor with a pillow and allow herself to start fully crying, muffling the sound so nobody would hear.

Why was this man doing this to her? Had she been bad and this was a punishment? No, it couldn't be. She'd heard of bad children not getting gifts for Christmas and that they got bad scores in school, but she never heard of anything like what Owen was doing to her.

Anger started rising inside her, sharp and unpleasant. Fathers would never do such things to their children, but Owen wasn't her father, and he never would be. Where was her real father? He'd left her, as though he didn't care, as though he no longer cared to protect her, yet she wanted to talk to him, to meet him or call him – she was desperate. But she knew from overheard conversations between her mom and grandma that he wasn't picking up his phone. He was avoiding them. A new wave of anger now mixed with the pain that raced inside her. Her tears had no end. What should she do now? She was hurting so badly and still didn't understand why it was that she felt this way. Owen hadn't been mean to her, he hadn't yelled or hurt her, but she felt sick to her stomach. Now even his name felt gross to her. She hated him! She hated his smile, his voice – everything about him.

What he'd done felt wrong, but she still didn't know if it was wrong. Would she be upsetting her mother over nothing? She didn't want her mother to start crying again, but she also didn't want whatever this was to keep happening. The questions were pouring out one after another, but they only seemed to lead to more questions. Soon she fell asleep.

Three days later, Chloe told her daughter that, unfortunately, Owen had to leave for Montreal for some time due to his mother's bad health. It was more than obvious that this short separation was painful for Chloe, but Charlotte could not be more relieved.

That day, the girl went to school in a good mood, which was noted by her friend Zoey – a good mood was rare for Charlotte as of late. The classes were going smoothly, one after another – just a regular school day. In one of the short breaks in between, on the way to the girl's toilet together with her friends, she passed by Nathan. He winked at her, and with one fast move, he pinched her on the waist. She almost jumped, but not from pain. Everything happened too fast in her mind to track what had started first or why – her blood was boiling, tears watered her eyes, and anger that was unknown to her conquered her senses, making every little piece of her tremble. An almost uncontrollable desire to punch Nathan rose in her – no, it was more than that; she wanted to hurt him. He had no right to touch her, nobody had that right! She turned back after him and noticed that he was, in fact, awaiting her look. But confusion spread across his face when he met hers.

'Don't do that EVER again!' she said through clenched teeth.

Her friends came closer to try and understand what was happening. Meanwhile, Nathan's eyes were wide with surprise; this was definitely not the reaction he was expecting, but after a few seconds of staring at the girl who had gone all red with anger, he gave up trying to figure it out, shrugged shoulders and continued walking down the corridor.

'Charlotte, what is wrong with you?' Zoey accused her in a lowered voice because some students passing around them were still looking in their direction. She looked at Charlotte as though the girl had lost her mind. 'You've been so weird lately.'

These words struck her like arrows through her heart. She hadn't wanted to get so mad, and was it so wrong that she had? Was she the one at fault here? Was she 'weird'? Charlotte managed to control her trembling hands, and with a weak voice she said, 'I just find him very annoying.' She shrugged, trying to make light of it all.

'Are you kidding? Do you have any idea how many girls fancy him?' Zoey responded, launching into a conversation completely different from what had just happened. It was in this manner that the little group of girls continued along the way to the toilet, discussing the most popular guys at school. Charlotte was grateful that the attention was taken off of her. Now she was following the others, trying to nod along in agreement during their discussion, making it look as if she was totally fine, but she wasn't – she could feel it. The storm was just beginning.

At home that same day, she was doing her homework when she heard her name being called from the kitchen.

'Charlotte,' Chloe was too occupied, covered up to the elbows with flour, to go to her child's room.

'Coming,' the girl answered, hurrying in the direction of her mom, who was making Charlotte's favourite cookies. 'Yes?' she said once standing at the kitchen's door, inhaling the nice smell.

'Sweetie, I thought you could do your homework here with me. That way I can help you in case you need it.' Charlotte could feel more behind her mother's smile, more than a simple invite to help with her homework; she didn't want to be alone.

'Sure,' Charlotte answered. In truth, she already knew she didn't need help with anything, but she cherished the personal moments she got to have with her mother, especially now that Owen was in their life. And although she didn't like him, it was still hard seeing her mother sad from his short absence.

The child grabbed her books from her room and placed everything on the kitchen table, sitting herself comfortably in the chair.

'So where are you at?' asked her mother curiously.

'Biology,' Charlotte replied, not really focused because she had some other, not-so-school-related questions swimming around her mind.

'Great, I loved biology when I was in school. Is there anything unclear to you?' Her mother said, but she seemed somewhat distracted by her gloomy mood.

Charlotte hesitated for a minute, only because she wasn't sure how exactly to formulate the question, but she was convinced her mother was the right person to ask. Her friends at school were definitely not an option.

'Well, there is something ... When is the right time to start an intimate relationship?'

Chloe dropped the wooden spoon she had been twisting through the bowl absentmindedly, sending up a little white puff around her. It was just a matter of time before she had the sex conversation with her child, but she wasn't expecting it so soon. At the very least, even if her daughter's father, Will, was still around, she would have been the one doing the talking anyway. And she also knew she should be grateful that Charlotte was coming to her with these types of questions. Otherwise, it could mean an invisible wall going up between them, and Chloe didn't want that. Still, Charlotte seemed way too young, so Chloe decided not to jump completely into that conversation. She turned around to face her daughter and smiled a little awkwardly.

'Honey, where is this question coming from? Did anyone at school say something to you?'

'No, I'm just curious.' The girl shrugged.

'Well.' Chloe took a deep breath and exhaled. 'There is no fixed age, but it starts somewhere after turning eighteen, once you're officially an adult. A long way for you, young lady – many, many years to go. I suggest you not worry about it just yet, but I promise to explain things better when the right time comes.' She smiled more easily this time, feeling that the hard part had been rescheduled, and turned back to her baking.

Meanwhile, an unpleasant feeling began to settle inside the little girl's chest. What her mother just told her confirmed her suspicion that Owen should not have an interest in her. It wasn't normal, as many other things around her weren't normal: her father's absence, her mother's constant sadness, the strange rage she felt today at school. She was sure that another – 'normal' – girl would have felt flattered by Nathan. So many emotions and thoughts were flooding through her in that moment that she almost felt dizzy – so much for a child's mind and heart.

'Would you like to dip a finger in the bowl before I put everything to bake?' her mother offered, clearly thinking things far differently than her daughter.

Charlotte's felt a jolt of happiness from the question, so pure, so in her nature as a child, so innocent, that anyone looking on scarcely be able to imagine what was actually happening inside the little girl's head. Both mother and daughter were filling the kitchen with laughter, forgetting about the homework, about questions or sadness. It was one joyful, precious moment.

That evening, Charlotte had her first nightmare, one of many to follow. The story of each one was different, but they all ended the same way – someone was trying to hurt her, she was screaming from the bottom of her lungs, but there was nobody to help. Then she would usually wake up, all sweaty and frightened. She would light up the little lamp on the drawer next to her bed; otherwise, it was impossible to fall asleep again.

At school, Nathan didn't dare tease her anymore; in fact, he began walking past her without acknowledging her presence. She had become invisible. Maybe he had decided there was something weird with her, but the truth was that she was silent, desperate and hurt ... if only someone could see that.

But the problems she had started developing didn't end there. She noticed as time went on that the presence of boys around her had become almost unbearable to her. If she saw a group of guys walking towards her in the school hallway, she would find a way to change her direction and avoid walking past them. Charlotte was almost never alone outside home or school, but sometimes her mother would send her to the local shop for some groceries she had forgotten to buy from the big supermarket, and if the girl saw a man walking on the same side of the street as her, she would cross to the other side. Her fear was bigger than ever, and kept growing with frightening speed.

Her mother didn't notice anything, however. She was too busy working and dealing with everything she had to deal with as a single parent, which was not an insignificant amount – who could blame her? Add to this the fact that her focus was getting pulled on Owen, who was making her so happy that it was difficult for her to see anything negative in him at all.

Some time after what had taken place in the bathroom, Charlotte's mom had asked Owen to pick her up from school once again. This time, however, the girl was aware of it and had bravely decided to act in order to avoid being alone with the disgusting, scary man again.

When the school bell rang, marking the end of the last class, Charlotte merged with the crowd of students going out. When she noticed Owen from far away, standing in front of his car, she simply went to the opposite side of the street.

The streets around the school building were familiar to the girl only up to a few blocks. After that, she was walking blindly, but boldly. Charlotte wasn't afraid to get lost, nothing could scare her more than being alone with that horrible man. She was walking with fast, big steps, the cold air was tearing her lungs with every deep breath, but nothing would stop her from escaping. She had no direction, only a purpose – get away from him.

Suddenly, a strong hand caught her on the shoulder and made her stop. She turned around, frightened, to see Owen's smile up above her.

'My sweet Charlotte, this was a very dangerous idea. Walking around the streets on your own is not safe for little girls like yourself; you never know what scary things might be waiting around the corner. Let's go home.' Holding her hand, he led her to the car stopped a few steps away, left waiting with an open door. 'You should know, your mother will be very upset, and she has the right to be.

While driving, Owen kept talking, giving her a lecture on the unreasonable move she had made. The girl was staring through the window, watching the people on the street, walking peacefully, unaware of the danger she was in as she wondered if anyone could help her.'... But of course, we don't want to see your mother upset, do we? That's why I suggest we keep this a secret. And even though you were a little naughty today, I still have a surprise for you.' He smiled softly at her as he parked. In the back seat of the car, there was a box wrapped in pretty paper with a big red ribbon on it. He reached to grab it and handed it to the child.

'This is for you, but don't rush and open it here. Let's go upstairs.'

Charlotte didn't respond. There was nothing to do but follow him. When they finally got into the apartment, he sat on the couch and made signalled for her to sit next to him. The girl moved slowly closer but remained standing.

'Now you can open it. Come on, I want to see if you like it.' Owen was the only excited child in the room.

She began tearing the wrapping paper without any emotion, nothing from him could interest her.

It appeared to be another Barbie doll, but it was the male version. She lifted up her confused eyes and looked at him for some explanation.

'Wait ...' he said, seeming to jump out of his skin from excitement. The man disappeared into the hallway, and a minute later he came back holding the Barbie doll he had given her some time ago.

When he sat back on the couch, he took the two dolls and placed them on top of each other, lying on the couch.

'Now you can play with both. You can do different things that I can show you ...' He pulled her closer to him and tried to embrace her. Charlotte could feel his breath against her skin and pulled away instinctively with as much force as she had.

'I don't want to. Leave me ...' The tears had started again.

At the same moment, they both heard the sound of keys trying to get open the front door. Owen released the child from his grip, and a second later Chloe's greeting voice was coming from the hallway. Charlotte took the opportunity and ran to her room where she locked herself in. Her mother found it strange and hurried to knock on the door, but Owen's loving arms wrapped around her as he tried to cover the moment with a soft voice.

'Don't worry – she's just very tired.'

It was convincing enough for Chloe, and she left her daughter to rest as she needed. Soon after that, Charlotte heard Owen saying goodbye to her mother and leaving. She then hurried out of her room. Her face was red from anger – as usual, the bravery came just after the danger had passed. The child ran into the living room, surprising her mother who had thought her daughter was sleeping.

'Sweetie! What—'

Charlotte grabbed the two dolls left on the couch and walked by her mother, fiercely, giving her no answer. Chloe, however, could see that something was off and left what she was doing to follow her child.

The girl reached the bin in the kitchen, threw away the dolls and started kicking it with all the strength she could find in herself. It was as if she wanted to hurt it, to pass to it some of her pain because she couldn't handle it anymore.

Chloe gave a sound of shock and cupped her hand over her mouth as her daughter proceeded to aggressively kick the bin, now threatening to break it. She moved in, gently embracing Charlotte in an attempt to calm her down, and thankfully it worked – the closeness of her mother was exactly what the child seemed to need. She burst into tears.

'What happened, my darling? You can tell me anything ...' Chloe was caressing her child, feeling scared – she couldn't imagine what could have provoked her otherwise calm daughter to act this way.

Charlotte still wasn't sure as to what she should do, but she knew one thing: if she kept this to herself, soon she would burst like a balloon. The first words were the hardest, but once they found their way hesitantly out, the rest was unstoppable.

Chloe had slumped on the floor, leaning her back on the fridge, unable to speak. Tears were falling down her eyes, barely reaching her chin before another one fell. She had fixed her gaze off somewhere, on no point in particular, and was thinking of the past three months with Owen. How could she miss it? How could she have not guessed what a monster he was? How did she not see what her daughter was going through? Chloe, in moments of despair, had allowed herself to indulge in the self-defeating thought that she might not have been a good wife if the man she shared eleven years of marriage with had left her for a younger woman, but she had never asked herself, even in her deepest moments of self-doubt, what kind of mother she was.

She let out a cry, unlike anything she'd felt before as the last thought passed through her mind. What kind of a mother was she?

She sat for a moment with her hands covering her face, and then she quickly moved them to her daughter. She took her in her arms just like when she was a baby. Now was the time to show strength. These tears, this horror she was experiencing now, it was nothing compared to what her daughter must have been feeling at that moment. She hadn't solved anything in her mind, she didn't feel better, but she would hold it; she would suppress the self-judging and the pain for when she was alone. Right now, Charlotte needed to see her strong, so she could feel protected.

She resolved that from that moment on, she was done letting Charlotte see the pathetic expressions of someone crushed from the life of a single mother. No matter how hard it was, she wouldn't let Charlotte bear any part of it. From now on, she would be a warrior. She would show confidence, firmness and strength because this was what she owed to her child.

The victim inside her died that day, when she heard the most terrible thing a mother could hear, and a wild animal took its place, a wild animal ready to tear apart anyone in the name of Charlotte. In the next instant, Chloe's determination began changing, shaping and transforming into something else – aggression. Suddenly she wanted Owen to be there, in front of her, right now, so she could attack him. She wanted to spring at him with teeth and nails to scratch his face and those disgusting hands that touched her innocent child. She was going to destroy him, no matter the cost!

The next day, little Charlotte had been sent away to her grandmother's, and Chloe had asked a friend to help her pack their belongings from the apartment. No longer blinded by her weakness, the solution came naturally and quickly; she and Charlotte were going to move in with her mother and create a new beginning.

The apartment couldn't be sold yet as there were still three years left on the mortgage, and William surely wouldn't be moving a finger to help – he was barely paying child support – so the plan was to put it up for rent. It wouldn't provide them with any extra financial freedom, but it would at least cover the monthly mortgage payments.

One day she would sell the apartment, buy a new one and create new happy memories. For now, however, they had to fit their lives into the small space available over at her mother's, but it was an easy decision to be able to leave behind that wrecked home.

The packing went much smoother than Chloe had expected, mainly because she didn't need to move the furniture. Her college friend, Mia, was a great help and support throughout the process. With an extra pair of hands, the two managed to have everything wrapped up and finished by the next morning. Chloe thought she might get emotional leaving the place, but the whole thing felt more like a dream, one very realistic and terrifying dream. She had called work though, to warn that she wouldn't be able to go in for a couple of days; her expectations were correct in that regard she needed a few days to organise her new life.

As the two were loading some of the boxes into Chloe's car, Mia broke the silence, albeit a bit hesitantly – she wasn't sure if a question would help or upset her friend. 'So ... are you planning on telling Will what happened?' She shifted her gaze from what she was doing over to Chloe, watching for her reaction. 'I'm sorry, I really shouldn't have asked that. Ignore me.'

Chloe exhaled heavily and ran a hand through her hair while resting the other on her hip. 'I guess I have to … Honestly, I haven't even had much time to think about it. I'm still just trying to pull myself together out from that mess of a life, for Charlotte's sake, but Will – the piece of shit – is her father, and he has the right to know. Charlotte has the right to receive proper attention from both of her parents. She misses him so much Mia ... It breaks my heart, really ... She deserves her father to be next to her, especially during a time like this.'

'Of course she does sweetie, of course.' Her friend had abandoned her work to pat her on the shoulder. 'I'm sure he'll be as devastated as you are and hopefully come back to his senses a bit. In any case, I think letting him know is the right thing to do.'

Chloe smiled back at her friend in agreement. After that, there wasn't anything left to be said, so Mia moved back to the boxes.

A few minutes later, while Mia was closing the last box up with scotch tape, marked 'Charlotte's toys', the doorbell rang. The two friends exchanged looks, but neither moved – Chloe wasn't expecting any guests. The doorbell rang out again, and she tried to guess who it might be. The third ring was short and was followed by a familiar voice.

'Chloe, honey, are you at home?' It was Owen.

Chloe's face flooded to a shade of red from the waves of anger boiling inside her. Mia quickly moved to her friend and placed a hand on her shoulder to hold her back for a moment.

'Breathe, Chloe – pull yourself together. We need to think; he might be dangerous! We don't know what he's capable of,' she whispered, hoping he might just leave if he continued to think nobody was home.

'He doesn't know what *I'm* capable of,' Chloe said, more to herself. She shook herself free from her friend's grip and moved to the front door. She opened the door, and there he was, with the same soft smile and a bouquet.

'Ah, there you are! For a moment there I thought you weren't home. I was worried about you; you missed work today and didn't reply to my messages, so I decided to come as soon as possible. Is everything alright?' he asked with a concerned look.

Chloe was standing at the threshold, showing no intention of letting him in. She wasn't even listening to him, just watching his creepy face move. This was the mask he wore in front of the world, stuck there, glued on like a second skin. It was hard to notice, but now Chloe could see the crust around the edges. She wondered if he was used to it now, if he even took it off when he did the terrible things that he did ... She felt sick.

'What's wrong honey?' he asked, his mask wrinkling, looking like someone concerned.

'I'm going to kill you ...' she said quietly, almost silently, through her clenched jaw. Her body started trembling from the rage rising within. Mia suddenly appeared behind her friend's back, and from Owen's shift in expression, that seemed to confuse him even more than Chloe's demeanour.

'What ...' he started, but couldn't finish.

'I'll kill you!' Chloe now shouted from the bottom of her lungs, her voice echoing at eerie, queer angles in the house's hallway. She reached out, and before Owen seemed able to grasp what was happening, she slapped him. 'Monster!' she reached out a second time and he only just managed to get the bouquet between the hand and his face. 'Freak!' She kept screaming while Owen looked on innocently, seeming to not understand her behaviour.

'Honey, did Charlotte say something to you? Whatever she told you, it's a lie. You know children have wild imaginations ...' he started, trying to justify himself, but this only made things worse.

Chloe threw herself at him like a madwoman, hitting whatever part of his body she could, making sounds, a mixture of crying and screaming. Mia had wrapped her hands around the waist of her friend, trying to pull her back into the apartment.

'Get out of here! Leave, or we'll call the police,' Mia yelled at him, and that seemed to add a bit more gravity to the situation for Owen. He turned around and hurried towards the exit of the building.

Mia had finally managed to get Chloe back inside, who was now curled on the floor crying inconsolably. Her friend kneeled down next to her and started caressing her.

'He's gone. It's all finished ...' she said in a soft, calming voice. 'But I do think you should inform the police right away. I'll come with you to the station. I can confirm as a witness. He needs to be made to own what he did – he must be punished!'

Chloe was nodding along to her friend's advice while wiping the tears from her face. She stood up and reached for the phone ...

That day passed, but the same could hardly be said for the memory. Despite doing all that could be done – moving out of the apartment, and pressing charges against Owen – the most difficult part was still ahead, for both mother and child to overcome the horror of the experience.

Every time Chloe looked at her little girl, she felt like crying. She was afraid that her daughter would hate her and would forever blame her for what had happened. The fear of seeing a reproach in her child's eyes was a pain that beat like a living wound. Chloe desperately wished for a way to punish herself; she felt she deserved it no less than that monster. She had betrayed her daughter by failing to fulfil her mother's duty to protect Charlotte. Now she would have to live in this nightmare until the end of her life.

Olivia tried to comfort her, saying that all would pass. That it would be like another stage of life, moving on like all the rest, and that soon they would be on their feet again. In that moment, it was difficult for Chloe to tell if these were just words or the truth itself. Time would tell.

Charlotte, at first, was feeling relieved from the whole situation. But that relief ended up being a bit superficial. The fear she'd felt back at their apartment, back when Owen was around, never fully left even though everything else had. The fear seemed to be stuck inside her, and it actually seemed to be growing with every passing day. Her mother was giving her a lot of her time now. She was helping with homework, asking how her day went, and even leaving work early to pick her up from school. Charlotte knew the reason; she could see the same fear in her mother's eyes, and this made things even harder for her. Everything felt even less normal now – the split of her parents, the huge gap her father's absence had left in her heart, the crazy man invading their lives and stealing the last piece of happiness left there, and the fear that they were both now living with. None of it was normal, and yet it was a fact.

Charlotte now found herself wondering if it could get any worse. She would often overhear conversations between her mom and grandmother, and she came to understand that Owen had been put under investigation and was also stopped from going to work because he wasn't allowed near her mother – near any of them. The case against him was going slowly, but successfully, according to her mother. These small conversations about the case going well were the only times Charlotte heard her mother sound cheerful. For the rest of the time, her mom's smiles felt forced, like a mask she would wear only for her. But Charlotte knew her mother was suffering, probably even more than herself.

In fact, while at home, Charlotte rarely thought of what had happened to her. She was tortured, however, by the lack of interest from her father; he never came to look in on her and ask if she was alright. She found herself wondering if he would care even if she died. This hurt her even more than the fact that he'd left them.

A week after they had moved to live with her grandmother, Charlotte happened to overhear a phone conversation between her mother and what seemed to be her father. Despite her mother's efforts to ensure that she was alone, Charlotte had passed by on her way to the bathroom at that same moment and stopped to listen. She didn't even have to press her ear against the door to be able to hear better; her mother was yelling so loudly that the neighbours probably didn't even have trouble hearing.

'How dare me? How dare *you!* You accuse me of being a bad mother when you've completely failed as a father. I'm here every day, picking up the pieces of your daughter's broken heart. I'm raising her alone and I'm doing it the best that I can.' A short silence followed, and Charlotte assumed her father was talking. Whatever he was saying only seemed to make things worse.

'Well, if you were there in the first place – at home, where you were supposed to be, this would never have happened! Your daughter needed you – she still needs you. I needed you. But no, you had to run off with your little missy, forgetting about everyone you claimed to love before. You've never called Charlotte, not once! Nice example you're setting there for her. Preparing her for the difficulties of *real* life, is that it? Well, nicely done. Now she knows that men are trash, like her father and that monster who ...' Her mother broke into tears. Her cry felt like more than crying; it felt like pain – all of her pain. It was particularly hard for Charlotte to hear.

Her father must have said something again, and that stopped the crying for a moment, 'What? Take her from me? You haven't cared about her at all since you left. GO TO HELL!'

The last words were accompanied by the sound of something hitting the floor. Charlotte covered her mouth so as not to make a sound, guessing that her mother had thrown her phone. She was scared. Why couldn't the bad things just stop happening?

At that moment, Olivia came in through the front door, back from shopping, and found Charlotte looking scared while the sound of her daughter's crying filled the house. Olivia rushed into the room and found Chloe sitting on the floor, tears pouring down her face.

'What happened my dear, tell me?' the old woman sat down next to her daughter and pressed Chloe's head to her chest as though she was a little girl to be comforted.

'He said that if this had happened before the divorce, he would have claimed custody over Charlotte because I'm incapable of being a mother. Can you imagine? Me incapable? When everything I do is for her, for my little girl...'

The words were coming uneasily because of the sobbing, but they were enough for Charlotte to more or less understand the whole conversation between her parents. But she couldn't understand why her father would say such a thing when he never actually called her, not even now, knowing what had happened to her.

Everything seemed so messed up and broken, broken into thousands of pieces all scattered here and there. Each night would bring its own unique nightmare. At school, she was trying everything she could just to appear 'normal' in front of her friends. She would never speak to boys, avoiding all possible contact, and she continued to change directions if there was a man on the street …

She was eleven years old.

Three years later

The mortgage was finally successfully paid, and Chloe could breathe peacefully. Finally, with great enthusiasm, she could sell the old apartment and buy a brand new one for her and her daughter. During the last couple of years, they had shared Olivia's home, which was way too small for that many people, but at last they could search out and enjoy their own space. Chloe was feeling light as a feather, walking boldly on the street, a smile stuck on her face; it seemed that after all they had been through, finally, everything was getting back to normal and things were moving in their favour. She had been promoted to a manager in the factory where she had been working, which meant she no longer depended on the money sent monthly by her ex-husband, William, for the care of their daughter. She also no longer cried about him; in fact, she didn't want him in their lives at all any longer – he had proved useless as a man, a husband, and a father.

A rumour had reached her that his relationship with the young, sexy girlfriend wasn't going as smoothly as it started. This was admittedly soothing to her hurt ego – trash like him wasn't suitable for anyone as far as she was concerned.

As for the problem with Owen, he was arrested long ago and accused of paedophilia. The police had searched his apartment and found tons of video tapes with child porn, which greatly helped with the charges pressed against him. His sentence was not as harsh as he deserved – a few years in prison felt like a joke to Chloe. Even death wouldn't be enough punishment for him. But at least she knew they wouldn't cross paths on the street for quite some time.

Charlotte was fourteen years old now and standing squarely in the teenage phase of life; she had become a little woman. Her period had started, her breasts were growing, and she even possessed her first pair of high-heeled shoes for occasions.

Despite all these physical changes, however, something remained the same, something she was passing from childhood to maturity, something that, with time, seemed even harder to forget, to run away from, to leave buried in the past ... It was chasing her, not Owen, but the fear. The fear of someone's look, desire ... or a will to hurt her.

Charlotte's friends had already started using make-up and changing their wardrobes to something more feminine. Charlotte liked all of these things that her friends were adopting – she wanted it for herself – but she was terrified it would attract the attention of men. She loved watching her friends flirting around with guys at school and spending extra time in front of the mirror in the girl's room. She had fun watching them in this new stage of their lives, but she could only bring herself to watch, and at times she felt a touch jealous. She wanted to be as free as they were, as fearless, but at night the nightmares would remind her that things were different for her.

One day after school, Charlotte's friends suggested they all go to the nearest park and enjoy the sun. It wasn't a bad idea for the last day of the week. There was no homework to worry about, she had the afternoon all for herself. They had just headed off in the direction of the park when a male's voice reached out to them.

'Hey, where to without us?' It was a guy from the other class, brownish skin and way too tall for his age. Charlotte had seen him playing basketball and knew a lot of girls had a crush on him, and she had to admit that she found him attractive as well. He wasn't alone; a few other guys from the basketball team were with him. They all joined the group of girls, making friendly jokes and laughing.

'Well, you were late, so we decided to leave you behind,' replied Zoey, all blushed. Charlotte noticed she began trying to fix her hair. Apparently, Zoey was nervous, or maybe 'excited' was the better word, and it suddenly occurred to Charlotte that this was all set from before. She pulled her friend to the side and whispered in her ear, 'Why didn't you say we were going to have a company?' Zoey frowned.

Zoey frowned. 'What difference would it have made?' she replied a bit sharply.

Charlotte exhaled; she couldn't begin to explain. 'Doesn't matter. I'm not feeling very well anyway, so I think I'll just head home. Have a nice time.'

'You were perfectly fine just a minute ago, and now, all of a sudden ... Look, the fact that you hate men is entirely your problem. You're going to die a virgin and single, but I don't plan on that being the case for me.'

The words hit Charlotte right in the heart. Charlotte had never seen her friend acting this way, it felt decidedly mean. Not only did Zoey not understand, but she didn't seem to want to. Charlotte's eyes filled with tears while she stared speechless at Zoey – she felt betrayed. Then she turned around and started walking to the bus stop. From behind she could hear the apologetic voice of her friend.

'I'm sorry, Charlotte. I didn't mean that ... Charlotte ...'

She didn't want to listen; her steps turned into a run. She was running, and her tears no longer fell – they were taken away by the wind. Was the damage inside her ever going to be fixed? Was the fear ever going to disappear? Was she going to be normal again? Was she ever going to outrun this nightmare, or would it always keep her chained ...?

Epilogue

Charlotte was in a hurry for her training classes. It wasn't particularly comfortable in the fully packed bus, but this small inconvenience quickly dissolved when she reminded herself that she'd be starting driving lessons soon. Yes, she was finally eighteen years old! She was excited, but that excitement would have to wait until next week; she had something else to be anxious about.

She opened the doors to the training room, and the relief of having made it on time washed over her – everyone else was still getting ready. She did a quick scan of the room. It felt like such a big moment. Charlotte didn't want it to end.

When, exactly a year ago, she stepped into the same room for the very first time, she was filled with anxiety. She didn't know what to expect, but she was led by a feeling of not wanting to give up, a feeling she had discovered during her sessions with Dr Ella Campbell, her psychologist. Charlotte's condition had gotten worse between the ages of fourteen and fifteen, and her mother had decided to seek help. The girl didn't repel the idea; in fact, she considered it helpful. She really needed to talk with someone outside of the family circle.

Dr Ella was an extremely kind middle-aged woman who managed to win Charlotte's trust, even as a friend. They had developed a strong patient-therapist relationship, which had helped in the healing process. After a year, Charlotte was a completely different person, something resembling the one she probably would have been if none of this had happened to her in the first place.

The pain from the abandonment of her father had grown into anger against him, but now they had finally untangled that knot, allowing her to see those memories as simple facts, as things that happened. There were no more stories about what it all meant about her. She had even forgiven him, which Dr Ella said was an excellent start.

As for Owen, the therapy required a bit more than just forgiveness. Charlotte understood that if she was to heal, it would be up to her in the end; Her mother, her grandmother, not even the psychologist could do it for her, but they were there to help. The power to overcome it was all in her, and she had to truly want it. She had to want a healthy life, without the frightening nightmares, a life where the closeness between two people was something beautiful, something wanted from both sides.

The solution wasn't a matter of suppressing the memory; it was always going to be there, but her relationship to the memory could change. This way it wouldn't get the better of her sleeping schedule and serve as a hefty obstacle in every interaction she attempted with the opposite sex. She had to admit that she was a good person, and even though she was a good person, a misfortune had befallen her. Just as there are good people throughout the world, there are bad ones, and that battle is eternal. Some people became victims, and others, with a bit more luck, didn't, but nobody could escape life's trials. The obstacles were there to be overcome, to make a person stronger. That was who she wanted to be – someone strong.

Charlotte was planning on starting a self-defence course, and her mother and Dr Ella were more than happy about it. And so, with full support and a dose of excitement, a year ago she had her first lesson. Today, however, was the last one. Sometimes things must come to an end. She knew this, and she was grateful for what she had learnt, but she had found friends here, and, at last, the peace she needed – she would miss it there.

The lesson had just finished, and everybody was talking, promising to see each other often. The atmosphere in the room was electrified with positive emotions. Charlotte was just exchanging words with one girl, arranging to have a coffee afterwards, when she heard someone behind her clear their throat. She turned around and there was her trainer. The title didn't really suit him, as he was only twenty years old, but he was one of the best students in this fighting art, so he was allowed to teach. If Charlotte had to search for words to describe him, she would probably just keep silent. He was, with no doubt, the most attractive guy she had ever seen, but leaving that aside, she was also very impressed by his maturity.

Often after class, the group would stay for a friendly conversation, discussing all sorts of different topics. He had spoken about the problem of violence against women. As he had put it, there is no comparing the sexes – who is stronger or more intelligent – everyone is equal because everyone is human. A pathetic act such as violence against women only motivated him to keep teaching self-defence – it's not always possible to turn a bad person into a good one, but it is possible to try to defend yourself if someone wants to hurt you.

Charlotte had felt that the more she got to know him the more she admired his personality. Then one day, she realised that he was evidence of what Dr Ella and her mother had been telling her for so long – not all men are bad. Now, as he stood before her, she felt her heart speeding up and the sides of her face felt hot and were certainly turning red.

'Charlotte, I want to thank you for being part of my course,' he said, sounding very formal. Then he cleared his throat one more time and ran his fingers through his hair nervously.

'And I thank you for being such a good teacher.' She smiled in reply.

His lips stretched into an uncontrollable smile; then he closed his eyes for a second. When he opened them again, his eyes seemed to have found some new motivation.

'Actually, I'd already thanked the group; that's not the reason I wanted to talk to you. I couldn't say this before, because it wouldn't be right with me being your trainer ... but as of five minutes ago, I'm not your trainer anymore. What I'm trying to say is ... Would you like to go out with me sometime?'

The pressure he was clearly feeling cheered her up. She found his behaviour sweet, and the idea of being with him didn't repel her at all.

'Yes.'

Townsville, Australia

Hayley opened her eyes. The morning had arrived, but that wasn't of much interest to her, not after she'd just had the best night of her life. A smile appeared on her face when she lifted her right hand to level with her eyes. It was there. It wasn't a dream, a mirage, or her imagination – her engagement. A Tiffany ring, white gold with a diamond. She giggled and rolled over, lying on her belly on the spacious double bed, so she could admire it a bit longer.

Zachery had already gone off to work, and she was completely alone in his apartment now. They still weren't officially living together, although Hayley was spending most of her time at his place, but very soon, that was going to change and this would be her permanent address.

They had been together for quite some time – it felt like they'd been dating forever. She met him at med school, where she actually had no desire to study but had been pushed to by her parents in order to continue the family business.

From the first semester, he had his eye on her, and since then, Hayley had been going to her daily classes way much more enthusiasm. Zachery was a year older than her, which meant he was in the next class, but they were always able to find time in between to spend together – in the park, the cafe, or at the various student parties. Those were fun years. Their love was passionate and emotional. In two words, he was the greatest and only love in her life.

Now, after eight years, marriage was the normal and expected continuation of their fairy tale. Hayley had found herself wondering if Zack would ever find the courage to propose. Not to mention, he had been very busy recently,

44

with graduation last year and starting his own practice. She was proud of him, and of course, supported him, but her heart desired more.

After last night, however, all her worries had disappeared and new ones, far more pleasant ones, had taken their place. There was so much to organise – the dress, the guests, the flowers, the menu, and there was only a year to do it all. There was also her final exam before graduation that she had to plan into her happy schedule. But at the moment, the only thing she could hear in her head was the name 'Mrs Hayley Smith'.

Hayley got out of bed, feeling energised and full of optimism – she didn't even need her morning coffee. She felt like an overcharged battery that would explode if she didn't start doing something. It was shaping up to be quite a long day: she had to call everyone, spread the news around, and – even though it was a bit early – look at some wedding dress magazines.

A day before the proposal, Hayley was having coffee with her mother, Evelyn, after putting in a good few hours at the mall. It was the season of sales, and it seemed as if all the women had gone a bit out of control; it was almost unbearable to be in a store. After a while, Hayley and her mother felt tired; the decision to have a seat with a cup of coffee came naturally.

'I really liked that last dress sweetie. Would have been just perfect for tomorrow's dinner with Zack,' Evelyn said, showing her regret.

'I know,' Hayley exhaled, letting her annoyance show. 'That's the thing with a sale like this; you put something down and you probably won't be getting it back.'

'What do you think is going to be so "special" about this dinner?' Evelyn continued, clearly more interested in the dinner than the dress. 'Any thoughts? Because I think I can give you a hint,' she said, pointing to her ring finger, dressed in her own engagement and wedding ring.

Hayley laughed. 'Honestly, I don't know, Mum. Don't put ideas in my head; I don't want to start putting pressure on him.' Even as she said this, she was blushing. 'I know, love, but I'm telling you, that man loves you more than anything – I can see it. He's just gathering the courage to take the plunge,' Evelyn smiled softly to her daughter.

'I don't doubt that he loves me; I can see myself growing old next to him, becoming a beautiful family like you and Dad,' Hayley said, her eyes getting momentarily lost in a dream. 'But it just feels a bit out of reach right now.'

'Well, it wasn't always easy for your father and me, you know that. You might be too young to remember certain things, and there were definitely some trials that you weren't yet around for. And we still have moments, moments when life is testing us, individually and together. These are the moments that reveal if you've truly found a partner for life. It's about support and care, not just romantic love. Your father has proven himself to be the person I can rely on, and I like to believe I've done the same for him. That's what made us strong and has kept us together for so long. Thirty years of happy marriage, though there were moments it didn't feel so happy.'

While Hayley's mom was talking, Hayley's eyes were filling with tears – she truly admired her. 'That's what I want for myself,' Hayley began. 'I'm sure Zack is the right person; I know we can achieve that.'

Hayley's phone rang, and she began digging impatiently for it in her purse. 'It's Hannah. I'm sorry, Mum, I'll just quickly check what she wants,' she said, standing and moving a few steps away from the table.

'Hey beautiful,' Hannah's voice greeted her, 'what are you doing?'

'Hey hun, I'm shopping with my mum for a dress, or at least I'm trying to.'

'Ooh. The occasion?'

'Yeah, Zack said he wants to have a special dinner tomorrow. No idea what's in his head. He might want to celebrate some promotion at work, so I'm trying to find something good to wear,' Hayley suddenly remembered the dress she'd walked away from and a fresh wave of annoyance swept over her.

'Wow, is he going to propose?' her friend made a sound that was almost hysterical.

'You and my mother are impossible,' Hayley laughed. 'For the thousandth time, I do not know.'

'Well, just in case, you have to look gorgeous,' Hannah said, suddenly sounding serious.

Hayley laughed. 'Goodbye, Hannah.'

The week after that day of shopping and the excitement of the proposal flew by in a minute. Everybody Hayley could think to tell now knew about the engagement, and the little happy bubble in which she was living was fully charged.

Hayley's friends had organised a ladies' night that evening at their favourite club to celebrate the engagement, and Hayley was at her place for a change, getting ready for what was sure to be a fun night. The doorbell rang, and a second after she could hear voices.

'Zachery, darling, what a nice surprise,' Hayley heard her mother say, followed by the small puckering sound of a kiss on the cheek.

'It's a pleasure to see you. Is it too soon to start calling you "mother"?'

'Ah,' Evelyn clapped her hands excitedly, 'of course it isn't.'

'Zack?' Hayley poked her head through the door of her room. 'Is that you?'

'There you are, sweetie, I was about to call you,' Evelyn called back from the end of the hallway. 'I'll leave you two kids alone,' she added, shuffling off to the kitchen.

'Wow, you look ... absolutely stunning,' Zack said, the last words not much stronger than a whisper as his fiancée came in for a kiss.

Even though Zackery had seen her elegantly dressed like this – and at other times even a bit more scantily or sexy – countless times, he always expressed his admiration, and it would make her blush. This time she was in a tight red dress that came up to the knees, delicately hugging the lines of her athletic body, kept in good shape thanks to all the yoga and running she was doing. Thin straps accentuated her chest and her blonde hair fell in soft curls across her naked shoulders.

It was surprising to her that the thin straps managed to support her breasts, as she wasn't small. She loved the effect it had.

'Come on, stop it ...' she giggled shyly, but his comment and the look full of desire in his eyes pleased her. She touched her lips to his as he slid a wrapping hand around her waist to pull her closer to himself. 'Zack, please ... My mum is here,' she whispered, trying to get away from his grip.

'Honey, don't be naïve. She's perfectly aware that it's normal to kiss my fiancée. Not to mention that soon there's going to be a wedding ... Mrs Smith.' His words had a soothing effect on her. Hayley momentarily forgot about her mom in the other room and gave him another kiss, far more passionately. 'You see? That was much better!' he said, satisfied.

Hayley's eyes were sparkling – everything felt too good to be real. It felt like with each passing day her heart was beating faster and faster; she felt she couldn't possibly contain more happiness, and yet she knew that this was just the beginning.

'I need to meet the girls in an hour.' She looked at him apologetically. 'Actually, is there a reason for your visit?' she asked, remembering that she wasn't expecting to see him.

'Do I need a reason to visit the most beautiful woman in the world who will soon lawfully be my wife?' This made Hayley giggle again. 'I just thought I'd stop by and wish you a great party evening with the girls.'

'Oh, that's so sweet!' She was all but melting. 'And what would you say if, after the party, I turn up at your place with this same red dress that you seem to like so much,' she said, letting a devilish grin spread on her face. 'I wouldn't stop your hands if you wanted to take it off.'

'Well, it sounds like a great plan to me,' he said, running his hands slowly over her back. 'But this is your party; you should stay and enjoy it for as long as you want. I'll soon get to spend every night with you. I'll fall asleep and wake up next to you, the woman who makes me the happiest man.'

'Oh, Zack ...' Hayley gently caressed his cheek. When her finger reached his lips, he kissed it.

'I love you,' he said.

'I love you too.'

In front of the club, Zanzibar, Hayley's friends, Hannah, Sarah and Lucy, were already waiting. Dressed in short, sexy dresses and extremely high heels, they were ready for the party, and the scream they let out when Hayley arrived was enough to call the attention of just about everyone.

'She's here – the most beautiful future bride!' Sarah shouted without noticing how loud she was.

'Shh!' Hayley put a finger to her lips. 'If you're already this loud, I can only imagine what you're going to be like at my bachelorette party.' She was trying to quiet down her friend, but she couldn't hide her smile.

'Oh come on, stop worrying about these others' opinions and show us the engagement ring again.' Lucy commanded. Hayley rolled her eyes and lifted up her hand. Another loud wave of screams erupted from the group.

'You're all impossible.'

The evening was a hit. She was in her favourite bar with her best friends, who she'd known since high school, the music was on point, and her finger held the most beautiful ring, which seemed to shine even brighter now as though it liked to be shown off. 'I'm going to the bar to order another round,' Lucy yelled across their table, over the music and the crowd. She was already having trouble walking straight, but that wasn't much concern for the others as they were all in a similar state. 'No, Lucy, please skip mine – I don't want to feel bad,' Hayley begged.

'Oh, no, honey, this evening is for celebration!' she called before disappearing into the dancing crowd on her way to the bar.

'And I'm going to the toilet. I can't hold it anymore, seriously.' Sarah jumped from her seat and hurried, leaving Hayley and Hannah at the table, laughing at the funny way their friend was walking.

'Well, sweetie ...' Hannah began, finally having a moment to talk more seriously, 'how are you feeling? You know what I mean. You're twenty-six years old, about to graduate, something many people would give a lot to be able to do, and you have a gorgeous man by your side – intelligent, handsome, and getting richer. And now, your dream wedding.'

Hayley was glowing. It indeed sounded like a fairy tale, she had trouble even beginning to describe her happiness.

'It sounds too perfect, I know. At this stage, I don't think there's anything else I want from life. My feet seem to keep landing, step by step, right along my path. I feel incredible. Even though ... You know I don't really care about the stupid education; it was never my passion to study medicine. I did it because of my parents, and then I continued because of Zack – it was one of the things that connected us.' She shrugged, as though this perfectly articulated the rest of her explanation, but for the first time that night, there was a touch of sadness on her face.

'I know, but it's a good profession. Plus, I don't really think you're going to have to work a lot.' Hannah winked. 'With Zack next to you, you can just stay home, find a hobby, and enjoy the good life.'

'Yeah ... I guess so ...' Hayley said, feeling a bit uncertain. She didn't doubt if what Hannah had said was true, but she wasn't sure if she would find satisfaction in 'the good life'. She would prefer to work, but she'd like to do something she was passionate about.

The two women were then unable to finish their conversation, interrupted by an uninvited guest who had appeared right in front of their table.

'Hi,' the intruder said. He was well-built and had a certain charm to him, standing there with a friendly smile and a glass in his hand. His gaze was on Hayley.

'Unless you're a waiter, we're not interested.' Hannah waved a hand at him.

'I'm not a waiter; I just noticed your very beautiful friend,' he said without taking his eyes from Hayley.

Hayley immediately felt uncomfortable. Under the effect of the alcohol and encouraged by Hannah's mocking attitude, she followed suit.

'Ha, I think you're too confident. You'd better move on – you won't find what you're looking for at this table!' Hayley's words came out a bit more arrogant than she had intended.

'I ... just wanted to know your name and ... buy you a drink,' replied the man, now visibly uncomfortable from the rude rejection he most likely wasn't expecting. Suddenly, his apparent discomfort seemed to turn to

51

irritation, possibly even anger, as his face bent into a deep frown. It was a little hard to tell, however – the bar was dark and the two women had been drinking quite a bit. However, Hannah and Hayley found it funny that they'd managed to embarrass the stranger. They found it so funny, in fact, that they continued laughing at him until Lucy and Sarah both returned to the table at the same time.

'What's going on here?' Lucy said, shooting a look of confusion over at the random man.

'This intruder not only had the guts to come here and flirt but is also stupid enough not to understand when it's time to leave,' Hayley said in a mocking tone.

'Well, we can call security and they'll make him understand.' Sarah placed her hands on her waist, a pose that was meant to frighten him, showing that they were not to be messed with.

The guy turned around and left, no doubt hearing the fit of laughter that then broke out behind him at the table. But just before he'd turned to walk away, Hayley had a brief moment where she swore she could feel his anger – the look he gave her seemed like it was meant to burn her. But they had been drinking quite a lot, and Hayley felt the alcohol could have been making things a bit more dramatic.

The evening moved on and the little encounter was forgotten. The girls danced until their feet could no longer hold them. At midnight, Lucy was already so drunk that she couldn't even sit without someone holding her. This announced the official end of the party so they could get Lucy home.

While the girls all helped walk their friend out of the bar, Hannah muttered under her breath, 'How did this happen? Every time, I tell her to watch how much she drinks.'

Hayley started giggling, and they all lost control over Lucy, almost dropping her. It took them a second to get their balance again, but they were eventually able to reach the pavement to wait for a taxi. The fresh air helped Hayley clear her mind. She had stopped drinking about an hour ago and could now feel the alcohol starting to fade; she was beginning to dream of her soft, comfortable bed.

'Wow, that was quick. Apparently, the driver was nearby., Hannah called out as she put her phone back into her purse. 'He'll be here in a minute.'

'That's great, but I don't think Lucy has that much time; she looks like a total mess. We really need to bring her home.' commented Sarah looking sceptically at her friend, who seemed to be sleeping in a standing position.

'Oh, no!' Hayley screamed suddenly. 'I don't have my phone ...' She was searching in her small purse, but it was definitely not in there. At the same moment, the taxi pulled from around the corner.

'Do you think it's on the table? Didn't we check that we had everything with us before leaving?' Sarah wondered aloud.

The car stopped in front of them. 'You all go. I have to go back and try to find my phone. I'll order another taxi after that,' Hayley said.

'Are you sure? Maybe one of us should stay with you.' Sarah suggested.

'Don't worry, honey. You all get Lucy home – she looks like she's about to pass out. I'll call you later, okay?' She then hurried back to the entrance of the bar. From behind she could hear the closing of the car door, which meant her friends had successfully managed to get Lucy in.

Hayley practically ran back to the table where they had been sitting just ten minutes ago. It was empty and already clean. Perhaps the waitress had found the phone and left it at the bar.

She quickly managed to squeeze her way up to the counter and started looking around for the barman or another member of the staff. The place was still quite full, and everyone was still busy.

A waitress walked past Hayley, and she hurriedly stopped her and explained the situation. The waitress politely said that she would check for the phone and disappeared, leaving Hayley to wait.

Hayley was nervously tapping her fingers and biting her lips. Regretting not having asked one of her friends to stay with her. If she couldn't find her phone, how would she call a taxi? She could call Zack to pick her up, but this – obviously – required a phone too.

The waitress then reappeared. 'I'm sorry, but I couldn't find anything. Someone probably took it before we cleaned the table.' She shrugged as there was nothing else to be done and was about to head off back to her duties when Hayley reached out to stop her again.

'Do you have a staff phone I can use? I just need to call a cab so I can get back home.' She was now feeling desperate and it no doubt shown in her voice.

The waitress, a pretty girl, with a lot of make-up and a uniform, meant more to show off than to cover up, took a moment to think.

'We have one in the office, but that area's restricted to the public.' she said with a 'sorry' face and clearly no more time to lose as she headed to the next table and began taking orders.

Hayley took a deep breath and covered her eyes with her hands to help her think without panicking. How could this evening have taken such a turn? This was certainly an unexpected end to her engagement party. 'Are you okay?'

The question came from an unfamiliar voice and she picked her head up out of her hands to see who it was. With a surprise, she found she recognised the person. It was the same guy who had come to their table earlier in an attempt to flirt with her, at least she thought it was. He looked a bit different now, more polite and keeping a respectful distance. His eyes ... very calm. Maybe she had misjudged him – she partially blamed the alcohol. 'I ...' she wasn't sure if she could say, but she really needed help. Maybe he would offer her his phone.'... actually, not really.'

The guy leaned towards her, obviously just so he could hear better – the music was way too loud for a casual conversation. 'Can I help somehow?' Hayley felt honesty behind the question. She definitely had nothing to lose.

'Apparently, I've lost my phone and I really need to make a call.' She decided to give a short explanation.

'It went missing here at the bar?' the guy asked, and she nodded along in agreement. 'If you want, I could help you find it, or I can lend you mine to call whoever you need.' Hayley suddenly felt stupid. Here she was, about to accept help from the man who she and her friends humiliated earlier. He seemed like he genuinely wanted to help. She suddenly felt guilty and didn't want to appear even ruder by rejecting an honest offer to help. She could clearly see he wasn't some pervert or a playboy. Also, if she had to be very honest with herself, there weren't a lot of other options.

'That would be great. I think I'd just like to use your phone. I've already searched for mine – it's a lost cause.' She smiled at him, convinced she owed him the better version of herself since he already witnessed the one she was not so proud of.

He made a sign for her to follow him. When they reached the exit of the bar, where it wasn't that loud and they could finally talk normally without having to shout, he said, 'Inside is so crazy; it's no surprise you lost something. Once I was here with friends and I swear to God the same thing happened.' She was looking at him a bit confused, so he explained, 'One of the guys ended up without his wallet.'

'That's just awful!' She was shocked. 'They should tighten up the security here.'

'Since then, I'd rather not risk it, so I keep my valuables in the car – that's where my phone is,' he explained.

It sounded logical enough. *I might have to give that a try,* she thought.

'Sure,' Hayley agreed.

'Actually, where are my manners? I didn't introduce myself – I'm Max.' He smiled a friendly smile and stretched out a hand towards her.

'Hayley.' She took his hand and added, 'Speaking of manners, I think I owe you an apology for earlier ... It was really stupid on our side.'

He waved away what she was saying with a hand to show there was no need for an apology. 'Don't worry. It's understandable. It's not uncommon for a man to give a woman a compliment only to be rejected for fear that he might be a psycho.' He winked at her jokingly and she gave a little nervous laugh. It was an odd comment and didn't do much to help her feel less guilty.

'That's my car.' Max pointed as they reached a Honda at the end of a line of parked cars. It was red and shiny as if it had just come off the lot.

'It's nice.' Hayley didn't hide her admiration.

'Nothing special.' He shrugged modestly and proceeded to unlock and open the door. 'By the way, I have a jacket here in the back seat. If you want, you can use it to cover yourself until your taxi arrives. You must be cold with that dress.'

It wasn't surprising that he was offering; Hayley had her arms wrapped around her, not only because of the night air – she suddenly realised that she was completely alone, dressed provocatively, on a little side street of the bar with a complete stranger. Even though he was being very kind, it made her uncomfortable.

'Thank you.' She smiled back, feeling that she'd definitely judged him too soon before.

Max left the front door open and moved to open the back. But when he did it, he began to move quickly, and Hayley felt the pulsing pain of a strong hit on her head. The movement was so sudden that she almost didn't see it coming. Overwhelmed by confusion and panic, she was incapable of reaction. She just groaned from the pain, but there was nobody nearby, on the empty street, to hear it.

Another force then began to push her. Despite her resistance, he'd managed to shove her into the car. The pain in her head faded a bit and her mind cleared up; she began screaming and kicking with her feet. The man got inside with her and slapped her across the face so heavily that she felt blood on her lip. The pain filled her eyes with tears, but the instinct for survival and the adrenalin kept her strong. She tried to fight, throwing the strongest punches she could manage, kicking, hoping to push him back, but the position she was in – laying on the back seats – didn't work in her favour.

The man grabbed her hands and skilfully wrapped a cord around them before moving to block her screams with tape.

All that had happened in just one minute.

Then the man jumped over to the driver's seat and started the engine.

Hayley's tears were coming hot and fast. Completely helpless, the panic took her over her – her brain knew was in danger with no visible solution.

The car stopped almost immediately. It seemed as if Max hadn't driven for more than three minutes; they must be still in the well-known area. She began thinking. Maybe when he returned to the back seat for her, she could push him out if she got herself braced and ready for a good kick. She would then run as fast as she could back to the bar and call the police.

Hayley knew she would have to be extremely quick; a second could save her life or ... God, what was going to happen to her? The hope gave her some much-needed strength, and she got ready to put her plan into action.

In the next moment, Max got out of the car from the front door and opened the back where Hayley was now expecting him. With every muscle in her body tightened and ready to work towards one singular goal, she was ready to attack.

She pushed her feet forward with such force that she was sure it would work. However, reality quickly said otherwise. Not only did she not hurt the man but he didn't even lose his balance.

Angrily, he grabbed her ankles with both hands and pushed her fully back in. He then got inside himself, again positioned on top of her, but this time he did something else. Despite her resistance, which had all the effect of a child throwing a tantrum, he placed his hands on her knees and with ease opened her legs. Hayley was screaming, throwing her body from side to side on the small back seat of the car, trying to get him off her, but the only thing she was achieving was hurting her own throat with strained shouts that never came out.

He spoke for the first time. 'You were going to make me look like a fool, ah?' While speaking, he slid his hands over her breasts. There was the sound of tearing as the delicate material of her dress was ripped. The thin straps no longer held her breasts. 'You were going to mock me, ah? Am I not good enough for you? Ah?!' He screamed at her face. She was shaking her head in denial as if her answer could change anything at this point. The tears were blurring her sight, but she could still see his eyes – the same crazy look she thought she saw earlier at the table. There was anger, malice ... lunacy. 'I won't allow any woman to do that. Do you hear me? Nobody will mock me!'

His hands were forcing up her tight dress. Hayley was trying to squeeze her knees together, to push him away, but the effort was actually causing her more pain than anything else. It wasn't necessary for him to take off her underwear; with one quick move, he tore the delicate lace. The fear in Hayley was threatening to explode at that moment. She was so desperate, and it didn't seem like there was any place for hope. Until now she had faith that she, or something, would save her and end this, that the worst would never happen, but now ...

The strong pain of the penetration pierced her and she gave a desperate scream. The monster had stopped talking so he could enjoy his moment of victory. He was making noises of satisfaction, and along with him, his victim – noises of agony. It was one ugly symphony that, fortunately, didn't go on for long.

Hayley had turned her head to the side, and through her blurred vision, she could see the light from a nearby street pole. The pain she was feeling was all over her; her head hurt from the initial hit, her jaw from the slap, her hands from the cord around them, her whole body from the effort to escape. But the worst was the pain in her groin, in her womanhood.

Hayley's groans started slowing down because of her scratched throat. She could feel how her energy had started leaving her, making her weaker and weaker ... She felt she might pass out – maybe that would make the nightmare easier.

Suddenly, the man got off her and out of the car. The nightmare had to have an end sometime after all. The next second she felt his hands on her ankles again, but this time he pulled her out. Her legs were so weak at that moment that she could barely stand. He pushed her down to the ground and threw something next to her. In the next instant, Hayley heard the slamming of a door and the starting of an engine.

The car was gone.

She was finally alone.

He had left her like rubbish on the street, which she knew was lucky – it could have been much worse.

There was no time for more tears. Her hands were thankfully tied up in front of her body and not behind, so she feverishly removed the tape from her mouth and looked around to get oriented. It was a small, quiet, not well-lit street, but the street pole with the label of the street name gave her what she needed. She was two blocks away from the bar.

Hayley stood up slowly on her trembling feet and tried to release herself of the cord. Her whole body was trembling from the shock, and she lost her balance and ended up on the ground again. Something next to her was shining, reflecting the light from the street lamp – glass, pieces of a broken bottle. And right next to it ... No, how was that possible? Was that her phone? She reached for it in relief and took along with it the sharpest piece of glass she could see. It worked well enough to help her get free of the cord after a minute of struggle. There was blood on her hands, probably from the glass, or the cord, or something else – she couldn't say. The pain was everywhere, and right now it didn't matter to her that much. She kept the glass in her hand, which now gave her courage. It was her weapon. She would use it to defend herself if only someone came close to her if only someone dared again to come close …

The tears started again. All she wanted to do was stay there, on the empty street, and cry. But she couldn't; the natural instinct for survival didn't allow her to give in to her desire at that moment. She stood up one more time, leaning on the wall of some bare-brick building and started walking. More than anything, she was afraid that the man would come back for her – she wasn't safe there. She had to move.

Still holding the phone in hand, she unlocked it and dialled a number. After a few rings, she heard a comforting voice.

'Hayley?'

She stopped for a moment and nearly burst out screaming and crying. 'Dad...'

Hayley woke up in a hospital room – not that she was able to sleep at all – but her parents had insisted that the nurse give her some pills for that. They succeeded in allowing her some form of rest.

Everybody was there, the girls and Zack, or at least, that was what she'd managed to hear of her parents' conversation as she was coming to. The name of her fiancée was mentioned a couple of times and that had caught her attention. While her consciousness was trying to piece together her memory, she heard it again.

'Zack ... I can't believe it ... Are you sure, Archie?' her mother whispered. Her voice was broken, laden with sadness.

'I'm afraid so, Evelyn ... Unexpected for all of us, but yes ...' her father replied, matching her mother's sadness.

'No! I refuse to accept that. I'm going to talk to him.'

'There's no point, Evelyn ... Evelyn ...'

She had already left the room, where Hayley was holding her eyes closed, pretending to still be sleeping, trying to understand what that was all about.

'Zack ... Zackery ...' Hayley's mother was running after him in the hospital's parking lot where Lucy had told her she might still be able to catch him. 'Stop!' she shouted hysterically, desperate. The sound echoed across the motionless blacktop, making it feel even emptier.

He stopped and turned around, his face displaying a look of horror, but it wasn't because of Evelyn's shout. She finally reached him, out of breath from running, and faced him.

'Where are you off to? Your place is next to her right now!' she started, but he interrupted her. He seemed on the edge of tears.

'No Evelyn, I can't ... I have no strength for that.' Zackery was looking at her and appeared apologetic.

'What do you mean? What is it that you can't? Have you asked yourself if she can? Have you asked her first how she feels before thinking of yourself?' She was raising her voice now, not caring if anyone might hear them.

'Tell her I'm sorry ...' A tear ran down his cheek and he began to back away slowly. '... and it's not necessary to give me back the ring ... I don't want her calling me. I only hope she will understand me instead of hating me. I just ... I can't look at her the same way after this.' Zackery opened the door of his car.

Evelyn was already crying; her words came out unclear, drowned in her sadness.

'Coward!'

He got in the car and drove away. Her last word still reached him over the sound of the engine, and as he drove off, he watched her in the rearview mirror, still there, standing, shouting her curses at him.

'... You're no different from that monster! You bastard! You won't find peace from this sin!'

Two soft hands came around to embrace her. It was Hannah. Evelyn leaned into her and cried.

'Come on,' the girl spoke softly, 'let's get back to the room. She needs us. No point wasting time on this ... trash.' She wanted to find better words to describe Zackery, but couldn't.

It couldn't be hidden for long from Hayley. After she woke, everyone visited her, cried with her, spent time with her, everyone except her fiancé. She asked about him, and as much as they tried to delay the bad news to help look after her critical mental condition from the trauma she'd endured, in the end, they just had to tell her. The doctor was present in the room at the request of her parents, so he could react with some medication if she had a crisis. Unfortunately, their intuition as parents turned out to be very correct. At first, Hayley couldn't understand the words her mother had selected so carefully to say. They had to repeat it three times until she finally said, '... so you mean that ... Zack has left me?'

There was no good way to give news like that, especially after a traumatic incident like the one she'd experienced. There was also no easy way for such news to be accepted. Hayley went into a hysterical crisis, crying and screaming, and when the male got closer to give her the proper medication to calm her, she got worse. They had to call in a female nurse to administer the medication because the patient refused to be touched by a man.

After a few days, Hayley was signed out of the hospital and her family took her back home. It would be three months before she left the house again.

Hannah, Lucy and Sarah didn't skip a day of visiting, and if they couldn't go all together, at least one of them was always sure to stop in. Evelyn and Archie were more than grateful to the girls for their support; it was exactly what their daughter needed to avoid isolating completely.

It took over a week for Hayley to start having solid foods again. Until then she was only having juices and fruits. After all of the exams, she was put through, it became clear that she wasn't pregnant, but she had severe vaginal tears. The rest of the physical damages were mainly bruises. Even though it all looked like it would heal with time, the doctor insisted a nurse visit Hayley at her home once a week and check for improvement or regression, but what everybody was most worried about was her mental health.

A month later, Hayley was walking around the house again, room to room, even discovering a passion for cooking, something she'd never suspected herself of having, but since she had refused to go out under any circumstances, she had to find a hobby to keep her busy, and cooking happened to be that exact thing. She managed to find joy in it.

Bringing up the incident or Zackery was completely forbidden. Nobody even dared mention it since the one time it had accidentally slipped out. Hayley immediately slapped her hands over her ears and ran to her room, crying.

Another thing that had changed was the clothing she chose to wear. Even though she was safe at home and didn't go out, she only wore loose, long trousers and blouses with high collars to ensure that even her neck was covered; nothing was chosen that would accentuate or reveal any part of her body.

'Sweetie, you know how much we love you ... we want you to feel better.' They were sitting in the living room, Hayley her parents and Hannah. They were having coffee with freshly baked cookies – Hayley made them – and watching some comedy on the TV. Her mother had brought up, not for the first time, the matter of professional help. 'We think it would make a big difference.'

Hayley put her cup down hard on the table and turned to her mother with a cold look set on her face.

'A psychologist won't magically fix the problem!' she said, not bothering to hide her annoyance. She could see the pain in her mother's eyes, and this only made her own pain worse. She didn't want to hurt her mother, she didn't want to hurt anybody. But she herself felt so irreparably hurt.

The pain she felt burned, pulsing as if it was alive, a living reminder that wouldn't let her forget what had happened, not even for a day. The only way she was able to express this pain, a pain that felt almost elemental, was in the form of aggression and anger, shooting uncontrollably at everyone in sight. She hated herself for that, but what was worse was that she couldn't seem to control it. It was a monster that would rip out of her, wanting everyone to feel the same hurt she felt.

Her next words came out like fire. She didn't care if the flames roared – she didn't care who they burnt, 'A psychologist won't go back in time and prevent the rape. Professional help won't give me back Zackery and make him love me again. It won't give me back the life I lost, the life I'll never have again ...'

The room was silent, save for the movie continuing on in the background for nobody. Hayley stood up and went to her room.

After slamming the door behind her, instead of going to her bed, as she usually did, to cry, she stood by the window. Looking out at a street full of people, her eyes filled with tears. Looking out at the people going by had become one of her favourite things to do. She envied them and the fact that their faces didn't bear the deep lines of tragedy as her face did. She wanted to feel her smile, her laughter, the light feeling of happiness and calm. However, the more she looked outside, comparing, the more frustrated and angry she became – she couldn't see how things for her could ever go back to normal.

The door opened. As usual, someone had followed her. She'd been out of the hospital for nearly a month already, and her family still wouldn't leave her by herself for even a minute except to sleep and go to the bathroom. They were afraid. Hayley could see it in their eyes, could read their worries – they thought she was a danger to herself. Maybe they were right. Why should she continue this agony?

For someone else in her position, maybe that would be a possible solution, an easy option. The truth was that, fortunately or unfortunately, it wasn't an option for her. She was a coward. She couldn't defend herself or keep the love of her life; she couldn't even put an end to her misery. She felt like such an idiot. Tears once again, after so much crying already, were following their burning trails down her face.

'Honey ... can I?' It was Hannah.

Hayley didn't respond, which was the closest she could bring herself to admitting she wanted company. Her friend came closer, and for a moment there was only silence, but the tension could be felt in the air – not from Hayley but from Hannah. It felt as if she was getting ready for something, gathering courage. Her lips parted, but no words came out, only a moan. Then she started crying.

Hayley turned to her friend – she definitely hadn't been expecting this reaction. Her heart sank; it was so painful to watch the people she loved suffer like this. Not to mention, Hannah was an extremely positive person, always cheerful, smiling, and happy. In their long years of friendship, Hayley had seen her friend break down just once when her favourite dog had died.

Hayley reached out a hand and pulled her friend into a hug.

'It wasn't fair ...' Hannah lifted her sobbing, red eyes to meet Hayley's. 'I'm so sorry, Hayley. This was all our fault.'

Hayley looked at her friend, not quite sure what she was saying. 'What are you talking about ...?'

'We weren't there to protect you! We didn't stay, didn't wait for you!' Hannah continued, now with pain visible in her voice. 'It could have been any one of us. It could have been neither of us. But here we are – we left you and it happened to you.' She was speaking more to herself now than to Hayley.

'Don't.' Hayley cut across her friend's line of logic, surprising herself with how well she was keeping her nerve as she tried to bring control back to her friend, who had lost it completely at that moment.

'I was there Hayley, at the table with you. I saw him! I was so close to him. I should have guessed his sick intentions. I should have called security ...'

'Stop. It's not true – it was not your fault. Get that sadistic thought out of your head.' Hayley softly pushed her friend, sending her to sit on the bed, and handed her a tissue.

'It's not your fault either Hayley. I can see what you're doing; you isolate yourself from the world, and all the while you sit as the victim with nothing to be ashamed of. You should go to the police station and help them to catch that monster!'

Hayley wore a bitter smile, shaking her head in disagreement. 'You've got it all wrong. It's my fault, mine and only mine. And it's because of this that I can't just forget about it and move forward. How could I with such a burden on my shoulders?'

'For God's sake, Hayley, do you hear yourself—'

'Let's start from the beginning, shall we?' Hayley interrupted. Her voice was flat and emotionless. 'We'll start with Zackery, who was apparently a terrible choice on my part. I let him into my life, I shared years with him. I was going to get married to him. While all this time, he never actually loved me; he was never interested in me as a person – even on that level, the connection was missing. But I didn't notice it. Now here we are – a knife in my back more painful than the incident itself. Zackery decided to leave me because I'm now "damaged" instead of staying with me "in sickness and health". As for the night of the accident ... Everything was perfectly planned. That freak had me as a target. He stole my phone so I would have to go back and look for it. He offered his "help" as a cat ready to attack a mouse, and I walked boldly into his trap, not even thinking about how odd it was for someone to go out to a bar yet drive his own car... It's completely my fault for being so stupid.' Her voice had by the end, almost to a whisper, as she finished telling her story.

Hannah obviously didn't agree, nobody would. Her friend had no fault for falling victim to a mentally ill abuser or for blindly loving the wrong guy. But how could she make her see that?

'I can't get my life back. Do you understand that?' Hayley's question was more rhetorical but gave Hannah the hint she needed.

Hannah took her friend's hands into hers. 'Of course, because you don't need it anymore! Sweetie, you don't need that life with a man who doesn't deserve you, a career you never felt passionate about, a tragedy that has the power to destroy you if you let it. You need a completely new life! A life where you're strong and overcome all this. A life where you can do whatever you like. A life where you give yourself a second chance with a man who actually deserves you.'

'I see him in my dreams. I see his car ...' Hayley began, but it wasn't in response to her friend's words. She was revealing what was hidden in her heart. 'Zack's there too. I call his name for help, but he stays still, no reaction – just eyes full of disgust ...' She trailed off as she said those words and broke into a painful cry.

Hannah started rubbing her friend's back. 'That's right sweetie, you cry some more. Get it all out.'

Hayley realised how right her friend was that day, how right everyone was around her, and realised that she herself didn't want to give up. It would be incredibly difficult. It would take a lot of time and strength of the spirit. She knew that sometimes she would feel down again and might even think that all her effort was in vain and that nothing could change, but more importantly, she knew that these would be the moments when she would have to keep going. That perseverance was the only way she could escape the black lake where she was drowning – as if being dragged down by something.

The days passed, and nothing seemed to mark the time; it was moving in the same merciless, constant progression under the eternal sky. The sun would rise, and people would be out there on the streets, walking in their own troubles. And there she was, Hayley, trying to follow the same rhythm as best she could.

Her family noticed a shift, but they kept their happiness silent out of fear that she might get upset and relapse.

Hannah, on her side, was trying to teach the other two girls along with Archie and Evelyn, not to treat Hayley as a broken vase. That special treatment was what was making Hayler feel different when she was the same, only stronger. Hannah was always described as the 'brain' in their little group, often as a joke, but here, in this unexpected life situation, she appeared to be the only one who knew how to approach it.

Archie and Evelyn were more than grateful to Hannah, saying that if she managed to help their only daughter overcome this obstacle, they would be forever in debt. This felt a little over the top for Hannah, but she understood why they felt the need to say it.

One ordinary morning, Hayley woke up with an idea. It felt so simple – she had no idea why she hadn't thought of it before. She didn't even go to the bathroom to refresh or make her morning coffee. She went straight to her desk, still wearing her pyjamas, and opened her laptop and brought up Google. Her fingers moved quickly, punching in a few words, and then she read, silently, still. She was strangely excited to find so much information on rape, and at the same time, disgusted. She wasn't the only victim of this terrible crime; there were countless cases around the world, some even worse than hers. She wasn't alone.

The statistics showed that in some countries, sexual crimes happen every five minutes, not only to women but to children too. Group rape of a tourist girl … A father raped his daughter … Women under systematic sexual abuse … A student killed while fighting for her life in an attempted rape … A woman kidnapped, raped and beaten to death … A teenage girl committing suicide after being raped ...

Hayley closed the laptop. She covered her mouth with her hands, feeling sick. This was a nightmare turned reality, happening all around the world. Thousands of women were living this way – now, before and maybe even into the future. She felt lucky, considering some victims of this brutality.

A sudden rush of adrenalin shot through her. She would survive. She had to.

She opened up the laptop again and typed something else. This time it wasn't a statistic she was interested in. Her family and friends had suggested that she talk, not to keep it inside, but she couldn't talk with any of them – they had no clue what she was going through. She didn't want to start therapy with a psychologist either – she couldn't shake the idea of sitting down with someone whose only awareness came from books. She was sure there were some therapists out there who had more first-hand experience, but something else was calling her. She had decided to join a group for women victims. What better therapy than sharing her pain with others who had an idea of how she was feeling, to see how they've managed to overcome it, so she could learn from them?

This meant she had to, for the first time in months, leave the house. And she finally felt ready.

Hannah and Sarah were waiting in the living room while Hayley was getting ready. When she finally left her room, she was dressed as she had been for the past few months – loose jeans, a blouse with a turtle neck and a giant vest. It was understandable, and nobody commented – small steps. She wanted to remain unnoticed.

'Well,' Hannah clapped hands together with a smile, 'let's go.'

That day, the two girls drove Hayley to the place where the meetings were held and waited until their friend finally came out.

'You didn't have to stay here the whole time, you know,' Hayley assured them. 'You can just come back in two hours to pick me up,' she added as she got herself comfortable in the back seat.

'Honey, believe me, if we had somewhere better to be, we would have been there, but unfortunately for you, you're stuck with us.' Hannah winked at her and started the engine.

It didn't surprise Hayley that they'd come up with an excuse to stay with her. They were scared that something might happen – a panic attack or something worse – and her friends didn't want to risk that. The girls had sworn they wouldn't leave her alone ever again.

Hayley went to meetings twice a week, always accompanied by someone. She could feel herself somehow lighter, and calmer; it was the best decision she'd made up until then. She met a lot of women, with different stories, and amazing examples of strength. It affirmed that life can continue despite terrible tragedy.

She started going out more often, not only for meetings but also to buy groceries and other daily things. In the beginning, she would look nervously around as if someone was chasing her. She was worried about bumping into Zackery even though he lived in a different neighbourhood. She was also afraid to see the man from the bar ... But she knew all that was just fear. In reality, it wasn't likely that she would get attacked at the small supermarket next to her home.

After some time, she started walking more boldly and hardly looked over her shoulder. It was progress – slowly, slowly …

Once, Hayley was doing her shopping, striking things from her list. She was struggling to find the flour, which she needed for the pancakes she was planning for breakfast the next day. They were Hannah's favourite, and as usual, she was going to drop by before going to work.

Hayley was holding a package of eggs, wondering where the flour could possibly be – they must have made some changes to the store.

'Can I help you ma'am?' The question came from a young man in uniform, a member of the store staff, who was filling in the shelf next to her.

Hayley jumped up and dropped the eggs, sending them smashing to the floor. It was a total mess. She then pulled at the ends of her unbuttoned jacket, trying to wrap it around herself as much as she could. Trembling, she began to realise that this man wasn't a threat – he was staff.

'I'm so sorry, ma'am. I didn't mean to scare you,' the guy apologised before shouting over to another worker. 'Hey Alice, bring me the mop would you? I've got a situation here.' He turned back to the woman standing in front of him, who was looking a bit crazy, and tried to assure her again,. 'Really sorry – I just wanted to help.'

Hayley's eyes were filling with tears, her hands still wrapped around her body. She had bitten her lower lip to keep herself from crying, but she was already feeling embarrassed.

The employee noticed that the young woman was more terrified than crazy, but he didn't really know what more to say to her. He made a small step towards her with his hands open, stretched out, the same someone approaching an animal to show that they mean no harm. 'Don't worry, it's not your fault. I'll have it cleaned up in no time ...' She only seemed to get more upset.

Hayley turned around, leaving her trolley full of food, and hurried to the exit. All the while, the guy was looking after her, mouth open in surprise.

On the way home, walking on the street, she couldn't hold back the tears. But it didn't bother her that people were watching – she didn't care what they might think of her. She was fighting her own battle.

She hadn't given up. Her condition had gotten much better compared to what it was six months ago, but there was something holding her back, something she couldn't overcome – the closeness of a man ...

Epilogue

'Hayley ... this is the most beautiful painting I've ever seen!' Hannah shouted.

'I still can't believe that all this time you had a talent for this and never suspected it.' Sarah got closer for a better look.

'Wow!' was all Lucy managed.

Hayley rolled her eyes, a bit theatrically, and stepped back to admire her own work. She never seemed to get tired of looking at it, almost as if it wasn't hers.

'You're all just being nice because you're my friends and you have to be' she objected politely, but she knew she wasn't fooling anyone – she loved the compliments.

Everyone burst into laughter.

'You know very well we aren't just saying this. You've got talent,' Hannah said, wrapping a hand around her friend. 'We've seen many of your paintings over the years, but the last few are on another level.'

'Well … maybe that's why they're going to find a home in the main gallery downtown.'

'What?' the three girls shouted in unison.

Hayley couldn't hide her pride any longer. With sparkling, tear-filled eyes she confirmed the news, 'Yes, they took notice of my work they like my work and offered me a space to make an exhibit.'

Hannah, Lucy and Sarah threw themselves on their friend in a giant hug. There was squeaking, other random noises, and more tears. It was a moment of pure happiness, happiness that had not been felt for a long time.

They were in the small studio a few blocks away from Hayley's home, which Hayley's father had hired for her a year ago. There she embraced her love for art and discovered her talent, which she had no opportunity to show until now. The push she needed, came from one of the girls at her meetings, Casey, who she felt close with since the very beginning. She told Hayley how she'd discovered that music had a calming, therapeutic effect on her. Then one day, a friend of Casey's secretly recorded her singing and published it on YouTube. She got so many likes and many comments talking about her 'angelic voice'. It then became a hobby. It all helped improve her condition, to overcome the depression and believe in herself again.

Her story got Hayley thinking about what she loved to do, and she recalled how much she enjoyed drawing landscapes as she pretended to listen in her classes in high school. She always surprised herself with how good she was at it.

Her parents, of course, couldn't have been happier to see how well their daughter was recovering. It had taken time and many tears, months and months of visits to her recovery group for victims of sexual abuse.

Then, one day, she came home with the news that she had just come from the police station.

Just a month after that, thanks to the information she had provided, which had completed the profile of the criminal, the man was captured. It appeared that 'Max' wasn't his real name, and despite his little trick of hiring different cars for each of his attacks, he had left quite a lot of evidence. The last attack that he made in the nearest town was his biggest mistake – he'd misjudged his victim. The girl had a black belt in self-defence. He managed to escape after she'd done some serious damage to him, but the cameras in the bar had captured his face pretty well, allowing the girl to point him out to the police. After just three days of searching, the police arrested him under very heavy charges.

The news came as a great relief to Hayley and her family. It had been some time since she looked over her shoulder while walking on the street, but now she knew, deep down inside her, there was something broken that needed to be fixed.

Hayley parked her car and made her way to the entrance of the building. A few days ago, with a phone call, she had made an appointment with the dance instructor Joshua Brown. She had insisted on a private lesson, which seemed quite weird to him, but he agreed to see her an hour before his regular students.

Hayley took a deep breath and then boldly opened the door. At the other end of the classroom was the instructor, getting the music ready. She couldn't remember the last time she let her eyes linger on a man. With great discomfort, she discovered that he was handsome. He was tall, and even through his clothing, it was obvious that he was well-toned. He turned around and noticed her standing there and immediately began walking over with a friendly smile. Hayley was standing still, waiting for him to get closer.

'Hayley I assume?' The man stretched out a hand. He noticed how insecurely she'd offered her hand in return and how quickly she'd pulled it back after the briefest of shakes. 'Well, if you want, you can explain your reason for wanting the private message,' he said, reminding her of her own request.

She was very brief during their phone conversation; she felt it was more appropriate to give her reasons face to face. Normally, Hayley wouldn't just go around telling random people what had happened to her, but in this particular case, it felt essential. It was the primary reason she was there actually. Hayley needed to accept the closeness of a man as normal again.

She gave a short explanation, without many details, but enough information so he could understand the delicate situation. The man's face had changed completely. Hayley searched it for the disgust she'd always imagined on Zack's face once he learnt what had happened to her, but she couldn't see it. She wondered if there was some other sign of disgust that she wasn't picking up on.

'Hayley ... what happened to you is horrible. It's horrible that there are monsters like that man walking freely out there. It's horrible that the number of victims is growing, instead of the opposite ...' He paused, and Hayley felt she could sense some personal emotion. 'My sister fell victim to the same crime a few years ago. It's a difficult topic for me as I'm sure you understand.'

Hayley looked at him with saddened eyes. She felt sympathy, but also something more. The shared story made her feel comfortable with him; it was almost a feeling of trust.

'How is she now?' she asked.

'She's doing well. Eventually, she was able to move on. She's married and even recently gave birth to the most gorgeous little boy. With a mother like his, he's going to grow up to be a great man, respectful of women.'

She smiled softly, yes, there was hope. Not everybody was the same – not everyone was a monster.

'I want to assure you that I'm going to do whatever is in my power to help you through this.' There was so much warmth and readiness in his words, his face so bright and pure, that she couldn't help herself but trust him fully.

Joshua showed her where she could leave her things and change her shoes. Five minutes later, she was standing in front of him completely ready. He could see she was worried, and he became a little worried himself, but as a professional, he didn't let it show. 'We'll begin with the basics,' he announced, and she nodded along in agreement. Joshua made a step towards her. The space between them was no thicker than a piece of paper. Hayley actively tried to slow down her breathing, reminding herself that there was no danger here; she alone had decided to come here. She had decided to fight against the last thing stopping her from living.

The instructor slowly placed his hand on the small of her back and left the other one floating in the air, waiting to be completed by hers.

Hayley audibly swallowed and put her trembling hand into his. She hadn't felt contact with a man for more than a year now, and the last time she had ... was the most horrifying experience in her life.

Joshua was watching her very carefully. This was not a typical student, but it was a regular salsa class.

A tear slowly fell down her cheek.

'If at any moment you want to stop, we can stop,' he reminded her.

Hayley shook her head. Her eyes held tears, but she felt strong.

Joshua didn't say, but he admired her. 'Ready?'

Hayley lifted her eyes to meet his. They were firm. She was ready. The moment was now.

'I'm ready!'

Joshua nodded with a smile. 'Very well. And now ... one, two, three, one, two, three ...'

Stockholm, Sweden

The last school bell rang just a month ago, and Ines Olsson didn't look back. She had been ready to high school and say goodbye to that phase of her childhood – no regrets. That part of life was over. Like a page in a book, it was turned over so she could continue her story. The scholastic bonds were broken, and there were tears among her classmates, but Iness didn't share in their sadness. A new stage of her life was ahead that had been impatiently waiting for – independence in the adult world.

Her mother, Stella, had always told her that there was no rush to grow up – once you were an adult, there was no going back. Ahead there was only work, work and more work.

Her father, Hans, on the other hand, was very proud of her; she was like the son he never had – active, brave and ready to fight back against any obstacle.

Iness's family wasn't very wealthy, and Iness needed to join the workforce more or less immediately, mainly so she could put herself through college – she was about to start soon. Money was an extremely important part of life, but unlike with her classmates, the whirlwind of jobs, finances and increased responsibility didn't scare Iness.

One lovely Saturday afternoon, Iness and her friend Freja were treating themselves to some cake at the neighbourhood pastry shop.

'Well, that's it – I officially announce that I am depressed!' Freja said with a long exhale, digging at her cake with her fork instead of eating it.

'That's nothing new. That happens quite often to you,' Iness said with a full mouth, letting the joke show on her face.

'I swear there's something wrong with you. How you can be so relaxed? Everything is changing, turning into a contest of who can settle their life better and find a place at a better college. Then it'll be about who can get the best job. At school, everyone felt more or less equal.'

'We were never completely equal, and you know that. Matilda, for example, always did her best to show off and she wasn't the only one,' Iness said, reminding her friend about their rich classmate. She definitely didn't share Freja's point of view on this. It didn't bother her that they showed off as she was always more focused on herself and her own goals, but she was still going to call it like it was. 'By the way, did you know that Matilda's parents bought her a new car as a graduation gift? Now she can drive to the very expensive college they've managed to get her into,' Freja said, a little bit of bitterness now showing.

Iness rolled her eyes as she exhaled. This didn't come as a surprise to her – it was kind of expected actually. There was absolutely nothing wrong with being rich – that was everyone's aim after all – but Matilde was arrogant about it, always parading her parents' money around. It was no surprise that some people found it irritating. The important thing at that moment, however, was that Iness couldn't care less and wasn't interested in discussing it. Her mind was already wandering far off into the future, picturing herself as a successful woman who wasn't jealous of some insignificant people like Matilda.

'Meanwhile, what about me and you? How are *we* going to travel to college? Public transport – that's how!' Freja was getting moody now.

Iness laughed and reached over the table to take her friend's hand and comfort her. 'Stop looking at the others. Don't think about them. I assure you, they don't think about you. It's important to focus on yourself and believe in your own success. Just like me for example – I'll have a car as well. I'm going to buy it with my salary,' she proudly announced.

Freja looked at her sceptically. 'You don't even have a job ...'

'Wrong,' Iness corrected. 'Actually, I do. I've been hired as an assistant secretary at a big company. I was pretty lucky!'

She explained in detail to her surprised friend about how she made a profile on a job-search website, and how she soon got an offer even though she had no experience. Freja was listening with her mouth half open and eyes a bit wide.

'So fast?' were the first words Freja managed to say. 'That's really impressive! I'll make a profile there too ...' She trailed off as she considered the idea. It seemed that Iness was right, as she very often was. Here she was, not wasting any time in depression, taking action, and the results were already showing. It was no wonder she was so excited and not moody like Freja. This news had a motivating effect on her – Iness was always such an inspiration.

The two girls talked a bit more about the unpredictable life ahead of them, and soon after, they said goodbye to each other. Iness got back home, exchanged a few words with her mother and hurried to lock herself in her room. She lay on her bed and closed her eyes, but not from exhaustion; she wanted to take a moment and let her fantasy run freely, watching her dreams come true as though she were watching her favourite movie.

She was imagining how much she would like her job, how she would prove herself to be responsible and intelligent and how she was getting such a great career start. For the first time, she would have her own money – not pocket money given by her parents – a whole salary! College, on the other hand, wasn't going to be much different than high school, but she was still excited. She's always been a good student and she couldn't wait to meet new people and create friendships. She would save money, move out into a small rented flat and be totally independent. She would buy a car ... Her imagination ran wildly and boldly, threatening to sweep away her delicate, naïve little world.

Monday arrived, and Iness was eagerly drinking her coffee. She'd never actually had coffee before, but keeping in line with all the changes of her new adult life, she decided she would try it. She was looking at herself in the mirror, nervously smoothing out her outfit as she wondered how to do her hair. She wanted to avoid looking childish, and she didn't want to look like she'd put too much effort in – it was her first working day.

While travelling in the tube, she looked at her reflection in the window. A woman, dressed smartly in a suit, a handbag across her shoulder, was looking back at her. She was proud of herself. It was real life, not a school that was shielding her from reality instead of preparing her for what she could expect in the working world. She was full of energy, feeling ready, even if she didn't know what for. The bottom line was that she would manage, with everything, because it all depended on her, not her parents, not the school teachers – her.

Her stop came quite quickly, and she merged with the people rushing to the exit. Her face was glowing enthusiastically compared to the rest – all bored and tired at the beginning of another working week.

She finally arrived, stepping into one of those huge, luxurious buildings that Iness thought she would never set foot in. On the third floor was the office of the company that had hired her. Most of her classmates, who always looked so cool during the school year, were now probably starting work in some cafe or the kitchen of some random restaurant, but not her. Her first job was just 'wow!', and she knew that this was because she was ambitious. She would show everyone how far she could go.

When she stood in front of the open office door, she saw the high working atmosphere. The spacious room was filled with small cubicles with people working at their desks. Here and there, people walked around with folders in hand. It was all so different from anything Iness had seen until now – very formal and serious.

These were adults, professionals, and for her to be a part of this, she had to look like them. She lifted her chin a bit and tried to make herself appear more serious, even though every muscle in her face was trembling. She was nervous but was hoping not to show it.

After a moment, Iness began to wonder what she should do as nobody had noticed her yet. She needed to get someone's attention soon; otherwise, she ran the risk of someone noticing her in fifteen minutes thinking she was late..

Iness gathered her courage and made a few steps up to a desk that wasn't nestled in a cubicle. It was visibly different from the rest, and it seemed clear that the man who was sitting there had a higher position than his colleagues. It was a middle-aged man, with rolled-up sleeves and a look of concentration as he studied something on his computer monitor.

She stood before him with a smile and cleared her throat. 'Excuse me ...'

The man stood up, and with a folder in hand, proceeded to walk by her as though she wasn't there. He headed to a door at the end of the large room, which Iness assumed led to another office. The young woman remained where she was, unsure of what she was supposed to do. However, thankfully, she didn't have to wait long for her answer.

Within that same minute, the man returned with a smile 'Great! Just on time.'

However, he wasn't looking at her. Iness followed his gaze and found that he was addressing a person who had just arrived. A young man, probably the same age as Iness, was now standing on the threshold of the office, just as she was only a minute ago. He was also dressed smart and was smiling back at the man with whom he was now shaking hands.

'Good morning sir, I'm Sven Larsson,' the young man said, politely introducing himself.

'Please, call me just Henrik,' said the man with the folder. 'I'm glad you'll be joining our team as an assistant.'

That last sentence shook Iness a bit, and she hurried over to join them.

'Mr Forsberg? I'm Iness Olsson,' she introduced herself with a smile. The two men turned toward her with looks of curiosity, as if she wasn't expected. The short pause wasn't left to hang for long, however..

'Miss Olsson! Perfect. Now that the two assistants are here, we can begin with the introductions,' Mr Forsberg said excitedly. He then headed over to his desk, followed by the two young assistants.

In the few seconds, while they waited, Iness had just enough time to think about how strange that interaction had just been. Did he really favour Sven that much more than her? That couldn't be it; she was sure she was imagining it. She shook off the crazy thought because more important things were ahead of her – she needed to focus.

'So,' Henrik began, showing them the desk with the two computers, 'as you already know, your duties are to respond to phone calls, emails and do whatever else I need you to. I'll mostly be having you doing prints and running up and down the office. Whenever you have questions, shoot them to me. I'll be something like your mentor. The company is very busy as business is growing fast. We're going to need you to be responsible, efficient and motivated.'

During the next few hours, Iness and Sven didn't do much else apart from follow Henrik's every move as he showed them how exactly they would be expected to do their duties. 'The first day is never something much; the real work begins the day after,' Mr Forsberg let them know.

The excitement was still in its full swing for Iness even on her way back home. She had memorised everything Mr Forsberg had said. The school had taught her many things, but one in particular she was proud of - she had an excellent memory. Confident that she would be brilliant at her job, she almost couldn't contain her smile. She thought she may have even looked a bit crazy, but this didn't bother her. It almost made her want to laugh and smile more, in fact – she was feeling well and truly happy.

After getting home, she spent some quality time with her parents, going through her day without skipping a detail. In the end, all the excitement had finally lost its effect on her, and she felt exhausted, as though she'd been running all day. Back in her room, she grabbed the phone and dialled Freja's number.

'Can you believe that? I have a desk and a computer!' Iness was jumping on one leg while trying to take off her tights – apparently the excitement hadn't completely left her yet.

'Yes, I can believe it, given the fact you can't work without it,' her friend laughed. 'Now tell me more about your colleagues. Are there a lot of cute guys?' Freja was clearly impatient to know.

If Iness had to be completely honest – even she knew her honesty wasn't going to be appreciated by her friend – she didn't really pay attention to her colleagues. She had focused all her energy on listening to Mr Forsberg. Something, however, had made a little impression on her.

'Actually, the position was apparently open to two assistants. It was a bit unexpected, but I'm going to be teamed up with this guy named Sven. I'm afraid I can't tell you much about him, as he wasn't really the talking type of guy.'

'Ah, I'm sure he'll have a crush on you ...' Freja was already in the process of making a romance out of the situation. Iness hurried to stop her before she got too carried away.

'Why would you think that?' she asked, making it apparent that she clearly didn't like the idea.

'Because you're beautiful and you know it. Most of the guys in our class were in love with you, but with your nose always pointing at the books, you never really seemed to notice. I assure you, it's not going to be the end of the world if you finally get yourself a boyfriend. You've always been too serious ... Chill a bit!' Freja sounded like a parent, only that the advice was the opposite of what a parent would say.

'I'll have time for boyfriends for the rest of my life. I can't deal with this now – I have so many plans! I can't afford to lose time to something so unimportant right now.'

Their conversation continued jumping from topic to topic, and the two girls were laughing, remembering funny moments, until, finally, Iness's dying phone battery told them it might be time to hang up.

Iness put on headphones, got in her favourite position on the bed – feet up the wall with eyes closed – and sunk into the lyrics of the song she put on. Amidst the words and beats that were sent swimming around her busy mind, she began to admit to herself that her friend may have had some good points. It wasn't that horrifying an idea to start a relationship ... but how could she do that now, when her only goals were to get an education and build a career?

Soon she fell asleep, finding herself in a dream that perfectly echoed her enthusiasm – she was a success.

The working week had passed almost unnoticeably quickly for Iness. Even though she spent only four hours at the office a day, she was already feeling completely confident about herself and what she was doing. Mr Forsberg was counting on her and Sven to do their duties, and she was glad she felt she could deliver.

Everybody else at the office seemed like nice people, even though there wasn't much time to get to know each other – the busy, moving atmosphere didn't really give many opportunities for small talk. A lot of people would steal a moment for a cigarette from time to time, but Iness didn't smoke. She found it disgusting – a harmful and useless habit. She kept her distance from it.

It was for this exact reason that she kept to herself in the office while everyone was going out for small smoking breaks. She was largely okay with this though. After all, she wasn't there to make friends, and everyone was way older than her. In the beginning, she had hopes of breaking the ice with Sven, but something in him reminded her of Matilda. He also liked to show off, as though he had something Iness didn't; she just couldn't figure out what it was. With Matilda it was quite obvious; she always had the latest model of everything. With Sven, it wasn't so clear. She didn't let this worry her though – she had too much ahead of her to get bogged down in these little things.

The first day of college lay ahead, another new step in Iness's life. Unfortunately, she and Freja couldn't apply to the same schools due to differing interests, but this wasn't about to stop her.

Here she was now, standing among a crowd of people she didn't know, in a sort of large classroom, but different from the ones she had in school, with a spot right in front of everyone, reserved for the professor. Iness, of course, took a seat at the front; she wanted to be able to hear everything clearly for her notes. She wasn't afraid of being a student, it was the thing she was most confident about and felt the most capable of doing. With the experience of a brilliant high school student, she felt confident that nothing would be difficult for her.

The only problem that weighed on her was the prospect of balancing lectures with work and the free time she would need to get ready for exams. Being organised was a skill of hers, but regardless if she was skilful in it or not, she had to make it through the obstacles. She didn't have much of a choice; if she didn't work, she couldn't afford school. She had to manage.

Everything was going according to her plans so far, and she couldn't have been more satisfied. She felt energised, hopeful, and full of dreams.

A few months later

Storm clouds seemed to be brewing. Something wasn't going according to plan. Even worse, something was simply not right. It seemed that the more she gave of herself, the more her efforts went unappreciated. Was this even possible? If you put in the work, should success follow? Was it normal for it to be so hard?

Iness almost didn't have time to meet with Freja anymore, but at least they were still able to have long talks over the phone. This particular evening, Iness was angry, more angry than she could remember herself ever being. She was pacing quickly up and down her room after unnecessarily slamming the door in her mother's face for asking her a simple question: 'How was your day?'

Iness dug out her mobile from her purse and dialled Freja.

'Hey! What's up?' her friend greeted.

'I'm pissed!' she responded without returning the greeting.

'What happened?' Her friend suddenly sounded concerned. friend switched to a worried mood.

'I don't even know where to begin. It's everything ...' The words were all rushing to come out at once, not leaving much space to breathe. 'At the beginning, I thought I was just imagining things, that this couldn't really be happening, but now I know I was right!'

'Hold on, hold on. Iness, sweetie, I have no clue what you're talking about. Start from the beginning.'

'I'm talking about the fact that my manager, Henrik, doesn't like me and seems hellbent to block me from achieving any sort of anything at work.' Iness had flushed red from anger, and tears began to glisten in her brown eyes. She wasn't sad, she was simply that angry.

'What makes you think that?' her friend asked, a bit sceptical. It was hard to believe that someone didn't like Iness. She was brilliant at everything, and on top of that, she was beautiful. The upset voice on the other end of the phone, however, told a different story – this was serious.

'Freja, I'm not imagining it.' She needed the full trust of her friend. 'I can't even count all the incidents on both hands. It started with little things, almost unnoticeable. Sven and I had the same duties, and I would always finish my task quicker than him, more precise – even though it was not a contest – but I was sure it was obvious that I was much better than him. But for some reason, our manager began giving compliments to Sven for a job well done.

'Everything I did went completely unnoticed, but if Sven picked up the phone – he would get a golden medal for it. Soon they started having lunch together, and it wasn't just to make small talk; they would talk about work. Not long after, Sven started getting different tasks than what we'd been hired for, tasks related to other aspects of the company. Henrik began training him for something completely different than an assistant secretary, for something I would have loved a chance to do as well, but nobody's giving me the opportunity!

'Today, however, was the cherry on top. Sven collected his stuff from our desk because he had been given a new one. He'd been given a whole new position, something like "assistant to the manager".' Iness then remained silent for a moment, biting her lower lip; the tears were now running freely down her cheeks. God was her witness. This reaction was not from envy – it was the pain of injustice. With voice now weak, she continued, 'I couldn't make my peace with that, so I went directly to Henrik and I told him I would like to do more. I told him that I'm ambitious and I know that if I was given the opportunity, he would see it … He interrupted me, laughing, and said that all I had to do was make the office bright with my smile and answer the phone calls. Then he winked at me and walked away, not letting me finish talking, showing just how interested he actually was in our conversation.'

Iness couldn't hold it anymore and burst into a full cry. 'I've never felt more humiliated ...' she sobbed.

'Oh, honey ...' Freja desperately wished she could give her friend a hug in that moment. She also wished she knew what to say in a situation like this. It was obvious that Iness was right, this was totally unfair, but what could be said about it? It had been a while since they left school, and now they were in this new world where everything seemed so different from what they knew.

She sighed and began with a soft voice, 'You know ... my mother always says that this world isn't built for women to live in it. That for us, everything is more difficult because this society, this men's society, doesn't take us seriously and doesn't want to give us what is rightfully ours by the law of equality. I admit that before now, I couldn't understand what she was getting at. Maybe it's because I wasn't ready, or because I was a naïve child, the same as you still are. Now, however, I realise how right my mother is. The truth and the reality are ugly ... but if you open your eyes and mind to it, maybe it'll be easier to live with it. Just accept that this is the way it is. I don't see another option ...' As she finished, she sounded noticeably saddened.

The end of the first semester marked the beginning of exams, to the great disappointment of all the students, save for Iness – she always passed with excellent scores and didn't see any reason why now should be any different. Even now, with her free time being spent at work, trying to prove herself in the office, she could still make time to study. She felt no reason to be frightened. In fact, college was where she presently felt the best, on quite the other end of the spectrum from her workplace. She had made some contacts, a little circle of friends – a few boys and girls that she really got along with. Every time they would meet, it was always real fun. The jokes never seemed to end; she would laugh so hard that the muscles in her stomach would hurt, Most importantly, however, was that Iness felt light there, at ease.

The office, on the other hand, had not met her expectations. There she didn't make any friends, and her hard work continued to go unappreciated. The saddest part of all was that she was apparently hired just to make the office beautiful with her smile, without any chance of doing something more.

For a while now, she was able to work for just a few hours a day, and this would allow her to pay for school and still be able to study and attend lectures – all while ideally being able to save a little – but she soon realised that she was barely making enough to cover her college expenses as it was. The dream of a car was far away – she couldn't even afford a second-hand car. She needed more hours or, even better, a promotion.

She was normally the type of person to get motivated by a challenge like this, someone who never gave up – if only there was someone who would notice and appreciate her hard work ...

The rain started pouring seemingly out of nowhere; Iness hadn't bothered to grab an umbrella, and the distance from the underground station to the college was enough to get her pretty thoroughly wet. The day wasn't starting too well, but she was still convinced it would end well – with her brilliant performance on the exam.

Her friends were waiting in the hallway along with the other students from class, in front of the professor's office. Everybody was holding books and notes, reading for the last time before the big exam. Mr Karl Bengsttone, their professor – a not-so-tall man with a little, round belly and some grey hair here and there – had made a name of himself as being very strict. He had announced that his exam, contrary to many other professors, would not be an oral exam. Everyone would have no more than ten minutes to speak on a topic chosen by him.

The tension in the hallway was growing, and the collective conversation of everyone sounded like bees humming. The door opened and everyone went completely silence. The first student was called in, officially marking the beginning of the exam.

'I don't know what's worse, to be the first one or the last one?' Ingrid said, nervously biting at the nail on her thumb.

Iness gently slapped her on the hand. 'How many times do I have to tell you to stop biting your nails?' She was being serious, but could keep a smile from spreading.

'I know, I know … but I'm too worried. Are you not?'

'She's going to have the only high score in class,' Gustav laughed. 'You'll see.'

Iness rolled her eyes; she was getting tired of that joke, but her full lips stayed stretched in a smile. It was hard for her to hide her confidence in her success.

'I'm sure that we're all going to pass successfully, this and any following exam. Trust me. In the end, we're going to laugh about how worried everyone was. It's going to be much easier than we're expecting; I'm sure of it. The only problem now is the unknown.' She shrugged, making it seem even more trivial.

'Exactly!' shouted Astrid, who until then was leaning on the wall, playing with her hair. She clapped her hands, illuminated by the idea. 'I suggest we ask everyone who gets out of the room what topic they had to talk about. This way we can cross it off and concentrate on the rest. Brilliant plan!'

Before they could respond to her enthusiasm, the door opened again. The first student, a well built, tall guy, walked out with a satisfied smile as Mr Bengsttone announced the name of the next student to go in.

'Iness Olsson.'

Something seemed to flinch inside her all of a sudden, a slight worry. She quickly reminded herself that it was normal to feel a little worried, and after many wishes of good luck from her friends, she walked into the office. She didn't expect to be one of the first ones to be called in, but the sooner the better. She closed the door behind herself and headed to the professor's desk where Mr Bengsttone was waiting. He greeted her with a smile and took off his glasses as if they were about to have a pleasant afternoon conversation.

'Iness, Iness ... how are you today?'

He seemed to be in a good mood, she thought, and this helped her relax. It would definitely be in the favour of the students. She suddenly remembered the guy who walked out just before her. He was smiling, which could only mean one thing. Iness smiled back at the professor and headed to the chair in front of his desk.

'I am a little worried; I hope I'll pass.'

'Oh no, no, no,' he made a gesture inviting her next to him, 'your place will be right here.'

He stretched out a hand and dragged a chair nearby. He placed it next to his and tapped on it, inviting her to sit. Iness blinked a few times, a bit confused, but eventually did what she was asked. It didn't really matter to her where she sat; the important thing was to speak on the assigned topic. If the professor wanted her to change chairs, she saw no harm in it.

She sat comfortably but was honestly a little disturbed by how close she was to Mr Bengsttone. The only logical way she could explain it to herself was that this way he could hear her better.

'Iness, I have noticed you in my class, as an unordinary young lady – intelligent, with great knowledge. There's no need for you to have any worry about this exam. You have all the skills to pass it.' He winked at her.

Even though she was flattered by the compliments and for him showing her deserved appreciation, the little, playful gesture at the end didn't feel very appropriate. It actually reminded her a bit of her manager, Henrik. He had also winked at her once, underestimating her as a beautiful doll, incapable of anything. If he could only see her here now. She had impressed her professor with her knowledge even before passing the exam.

'Thank you, professor,' she replied politely, blushing a little with pride.

'Oh, I'm grateful every day for having such an amazing...' He cleared his throat with an awkward pause. '... student.

Iness couldn't help but notice where he was looking. There were still drops on her clothes from the rain, and some were clinging to her breasts. She didn't have time to dry before the exam as she was called so soon. She felt immediately uncomfortable and quickly crossed her hands in front of her.

'You know,' he continued, 'nowadays, it's not easy to find students as dedicated as yourself. Most of them only think about parties.'

She was wondering when they would be starting the exam. She couldn't really find a connection between this conversation and the reason for her being in his office.

'That's why I am so delighted when I see intelligent young people. I'm sure you're aware of the unofficial title, "favourite of the professor". Well, it's really quite a lucky position for a student to find oneself. Not because of the evaluations but because of the possibilities that can open for them with a little help from our side.' He winked at her again, which was extremely unpleasant for her. Mr Bengsttone continued talking in a quiet voice, playing with a pen in his hand, 'I personally think that you are a very promising student, and I would love to help in your progress.'

'Thank you, Professor Bengsttone. I'm honoured,' Iness responded. Of course, she knew what it meant to be the favourite student of a professor. This could indeed open many doors for her professional future. It meant that things like this stupid secretary work wouldn't remain for long. She couldn't believe her luck.

'But that, of course, is not a priority for today's conversation. We'll have plenty of time to discuss it,' he said, bringing her back to the ground from the quick fly in the dream world.

Iness knew she had to concentrate now, as the main part of the exam was about to begin.

'Your exam, however, doesn't seem necessary to me ...' he said, keeping his eyes fixed on hers, meeting her confusion there. 'I can make it easier for you. We can just pretend we had the official part, I'll give you a great evaluation, which you no doubt deserve, and in return ... you can come visit me later on.' His hand slid to her thigh.

It was the most disgusting feeling she had ever experienced. Her whole body reacted as if it had been stung. Iness jumped off her seat and stepped back, looking at him, horrified. Her eyes were wide open, like a wild animal feeling threatened. The shock had left her with no words. She was just standing there with her mouth half open. Just like that, it all made sense. This was why he asked her to sit next to him, why he'd given her all those compliments, the promises to help her ... He wanted to present her with all the benefits to playing his pervert game.

Mr Bengsttone, however, seemed not to be bothered by her reaction; he just raised one eyebrow in surprise. Then he quickly put his glasses back on, still playing with the pen, staring at the file with Iness's records.

'To be honest, Miss Olsson, I'm very disappointed by your performance. I had expected much more.' He started writing something while Iness was still looking at him, unable to believe what was happening. 'Unfortunately, even the best ones fail sometimes. However, a second chance will be given to you in a month's time ... I hope you will be more prepared then.' He didn't look at her again, and she understood that she was now expected to leave.

Iness grabbed her purse and left the room, almost running. Tears were threatening to cover her beautiful face, now expressing agony. But she had to hide the emotion, to keep the tears for her room where she could be alone and cry until all her energy had drained out. She passed by her friends, who tried to say something to her, but she was already at the far end of the hallway. Once she reached the big exit door of the building, she pushed it open with all the power she had and found herself under the rain.

Rain. Now she could release them, the hot tears would merge with the cold falling drops. Her clothes were soaked in seconds, making her whole body shiver from the cold. It didn't matter to her. Nothing mattered anymore. It seemed that everything she was expecting, hoping for – all her dreams – was all wrong. The reality was twisted and ugly. This world wasn't built for women indeed. So unfair, and at the same time, so real! She was discriminated against at her work because of her gender, and again, for the same reason, taken as a sex target by her professor. Where was the end of this circle? Where could she feel protected and free to explore her potential?

Right before reaching the bottom of the stairs for the underground, something caught Iness's attention. She stopped. A young woman, dressed in a red raincoat, was sticking flyers on the station's wall. Iness could read the logo, written in big black letters: 'Woman's Power'. Instinctively, as if dragged by a magnetic force, she moved closer to read what it was about.

It appeared to be an invitation to join a feminist organisation.

'I can give you one if you're interested?' the woman with the red coat said, now having stopped what she was doing, smiling over at Iness.

The next day, Iness decided to pay a visit to this organisation after work – she had the afternoon free of exams that day. She found the address easily, and when she walked in, a bit insecurely, she saw a big room with a silent audience. On her way there, Iness wasn't sure what to expect. It seemed that she'd missed the first half of a speech delivered by a very good-looking middle-aged African woman.

Iness remained standing at the door, but listened, at once feeling deeply moved.

'... It is not possible to give an accurate statistic for the brutality, abuse and vandalism against women because the numbers keep growing higher with every second. Why is that? Does the law do everything in its power to protect us? Is there going to be an end to these horrific acts someday? Or will we reach a point where a person walks the street, witnessing rape and all types of aggression, and carries on, undisturbed because it has become normal, expected?'... For how long will the law continue to allow atrocities and religions justifying abuse – physical and mental? For how long will there be traditions allowing the sale of children as wives or sending women away from their homes during their monthly period? For how long will there be countries where children give birth to the children of their rapists because abortion is forbidden ...?

'... Society is built from men and women with different skin colours, different nationalities, different languages, and different religions. The underestimating of one over the other, the suppressing of one over the other, the humiliation of one over the other is against all moral and human laws!

'Humankind is, in fact, divided into thousands of smaller societies, each one united by common understandings and beliefs. Having their own rules and traditions is fair enough, but what about the societies or groups that act against human laws? The human laws: no matter the gender or race, a person is a master of their freedom and their choice ...

'... What happens when there's a small community of people with extreme interpretations of certain religions or traditions, where women are forced to live with no education – not even basic knowledge – or with no right to dreams or desires? What happens when there are communities where women are destined to be slaves to their families, to never fully experience life ...?

'... What happens when a big city prides itself on being modern and advanced, yet women are being attacked and raped? What happens when, in that same city, in one of those houses that looks just like any other, there's a woman crying, physically abused by her husband? What happens when in the centre of that same city, in one of those shiny, tall buildings, a man is chosen for a job over a woman with the same – or better – qualifications just because of his gender? What happens when in that same city, a young girl receives an inappropriate proposal from a teacher, or a priest, or another male figure in a position of authority ...?

'... "It's not possible to help everyone," someone might say. "Not every victim can be saved." Of course, this endeavour will be difficult ... but it's this way of thinking that appears to be the main problem humankind faces, regardless of religion or nationality. No matter the country, the nationality, the race, the religion, we are not openly teaching equality, not properly, but in the last decades, the female class has slowly reared its head to ask not for domination, not for superiority but simply for equality. It's unnatural and wrong for there to be arranged marriages between unwilling parties, children-brides, women brainwashed to have only one life purpose – to make children – women forced to give birth to the child of their rapist, or even be forced to marry him. The list goes on ...

'... One will say, "The religion is to be followed. The traditions are to be kept. The world is not perfect and we can't change it." Well, I would say that God and the rules and traditions created by man require too high a price for a woman to pay. No God, no religion, no tradition, no law should cause tears or tolerate suffering and pain ...

'... People hear terrible stories and express their shock. They pray to their god and then secretly say, "It's bad, but at least it didn't happen to me." And with this, they hoping the world will change ... We don't need a miracle – we need action! We need the action of intelligent people refusing to live in a world where there is no equality of the sexes, no equality of skin colour, a world where all that exists are differences – different religions, different gods, different languages, different nationalities, different skin colours ...'

Iness's eyes were filled with tears. She clapped her hands as loudly as she could.

Epilogue

Iness was just leaving Professor Bengsttone's office. This time it was a smile that she was trying to hold back, not tears. Her satisfaction had no apparent limit in this moment. She was walking fast and confident, but instead of taking the stairs leading down to the exit, she took those leading to the upper level.

While walking, she thought about how much had changed over the past month. She was no longer desperate; the dark thoughts had cleared up under the sun, bringing back her hope and her confidence. The light had shone upon her the day she joined the organisation for women's rights. The connection with all those strong women, of all ages – intelligent and unbreakable – inspired her. It set her back on her feet and showed her that the problems she had would not bother her for long. She would overcome them.

And here she was, taking the first step.

Iness was now in front of the director's office. She knocked on the door without a second thought. A voice invited her to enter and she walked right in.

'What can I do for you Miss ...?'

'Olsson, Iness Olsson,' she said, strong and clear.

The director gestured for her to sit but didn't seem very interested in her presence as he continued checking some paperwork.

'Unfortunately,' he murmured, 'my time is limited and—'

'I believe,' Iness interrupted, 'you'll give as much of your time as is needed, Mr Engstrom.' Her voice was calm, but firm. 'Because, you see, the problem I have,' – she waved her hand, revealing a cell phone – 'the police would be very interested to deal with.'

It could definitely be said that she was holding all cards – she had the director's undivided attention from that moment onwards. She told the whole story about being forced to choose between not being allowed to pass the exam or a good evaluation in exchange for being intimate with the professor. Today, when she visited Mr Bengsttone for the second time, the situation wasn't much different, apart from the fact she recorded every word he said.

After Mr Engstrom listened to the recorded conversation himself, he was more than shocked. He assured Iness he would personally take over this case and she would no longer be bothered by the perverted professor.

This was all she wanted – justice, not only for her but so no other female students have to be trapped in such an absurd situation. This was a battle, and she wasn't just fighting for herself but for all women.

On the way home, drunk on the feeling of having won this unfortunate fight, believing once again in her strength – strength that had been lost because of dishonest people trying to pull her down – she was already considering her next move.

Later on that same day, her friend Ingrid called her with huge news from the college – Professor Bengsttone had been officially released from his duty. Ingrid sounded surprised over the phone; apparently, it was kept as a mystery to everyone as nobody knew why it was all happening so suddenly. But Iness knew more than everybody else. She also knew that as of that moment no more female students would be humiliated, and potentially even taken as a sexual target. Now, having gained back the courage she needed, the very next day, Iness was ready for justice in her office as well. She had to try at least. She wasn't planning to give up without a fight for her rights, without making her voice heard – proving that she wouldn't stay quiet as was expected.

Iness had requested a meeting with the Human Resources manager and was now in Mr Lindberg's office, before the start of her shift. She wasn't worried; confidence was evident on her face. Mr Lindberg took his place in the chair behind his desk and started the conversation with a smile.

'Miss Olsson, I understand that this meeting couldn't wait. May I know what it's about?'

'I would like to file a complaint for the sex discrimination that I've experienced since starting at this company ...'

A week after the investigation had been started on her complaint, as promised by the Human Resources manager, Iness still hadn't heard any news on the case. Her hope, however, wasn't about to die so soon. She was walking to the office to begin another day, knowing that four hours later she would be walking back the same way to the underground so she could make it to her two afternoon lectures at the college.

'Iness! Hey, Iness ...' Someone out of breath called from behind. She turned around and saw Ester, one of her colleagues from the office. She had always been nice to her, but as her duty had many responsibilities, they rarely had time to talk.

'Morning, Ester. How are you?' Iness said after the woman finally reached her.

'You won't believe ...' Her colleague had the face of someone who had a big secret and was bursting to share it. 'Yesterday, after your shift finished and you left, the weirdest thing happened. It turns out that Henrik is the uncle of that guy – Sven – his assistant. They've been hiding it on purpose, and since Henrik had been giving Sven preferential treatment, it's being considered as a full case of nepotism – they've both been terminated!'

Iness's jaw dropped in surprise before stretching into a wide smile.

To be a woman is not easy. It never was and it likely won't be. It requires more courage than anyone could imagine. It's a battle. Not everyone comes out a winner, and many fall as victims. The truth, however, is that all women are queens, majestic, beautiful, powerful – queens forever!

Notes

This novella is dedicated to any individual who stands for gender equality, respect for every human life, and those who will never stop trying to end the eternal struggle with violence against women, girls, and vulnerable individuals of any nationality, religion, socioeconomic status, and age.

This book includes an extraction of original academic material I have written as part of my Dissertation for my Psychology degree.

According to the World Health Organisation (WHO), sexual assault is categorised as rape and is defined as an unwanted and forced sexual act which is a crime against human rights therefore is considered illegal. Sexual assault is a global issue with 35% of the female population experiencing assault in some form, and the statistics acknowledge a rise in this number every year (WHO). The amount of literature and studies on rape provides a disturbingly high number of women on a global scale who have experienced at some point of their life some sort of sexual assault (Angelone et al., 2015).

'Acquaintance rape' or also 'non-stranger rape' is a term that has been introduced due to statistical findings that the majority of women victims of sexual assault know the perpetrator on some level such as family member, family friend, partner, friend, fellow student or work colleague (Angelone et al., 2015). Statistics bring to the attention strongly related to rape myth fact that the perpetrator is someone unknown to the victim (Angelone et al., 2015). In fact, most rape cases occur in a safe zone, such as home, and by someone with whom the victim is acquainted (Angelone et al., 2015).

Intimate partner rape is a common situation where increasing number of women can be linked to spousal rape and date rape. Highlighting the importance of recognising and addressing sexual violence within relationships has been suggested by the research work of many international studies (Monson et al., 1996).

Attitudes towards gender role play crucial part in sexual assault taking place (Hendricks, 2019). Patriarchal concepts where the male individual should be dominant and initiative of sexual act, and a female individual should be subordinate are widely accepted beliefs and reflect negatively on a social community (Straton, 2002).

The misunderstanding that women should know how to avoid a potential sexual attack leads to the formation of stigma around the rape topic where women fall victims of both abuse and judgment (Clark, 2007). Misconception that marriage guarantees sexual act also leads to the fact that many women are unable to recognise the act as rape (Monson, 1996). Domestic setting, for example, provides the feeling of ownership and therefore security, meanwhile, for women it can turn into a prison.

Furthermore, in a family or relationship with strict gender role beliefs, it is more likely for a woman to experience a form of violence (Deitz et al., 2015). Often violence is not perceived as violence by women exactly because of gender role beliefs adopted from a young age and enforced by society (Samar et al., 2023).

Particularly in sexual violence if happening in a domestic setting women can confuse their partnership obligation as complying with sex without necessarily having to give consent, where men also consider marriage as a guarantee of sexual act, to the extent where consent is not needed as it is seen as an obligation (Samar et al., 2023). Such examples portray spousal rape which is commonly seen in many cultures including Western (Samar et al., 2023).

Leaving an abusive relationship is a complex and challenging process, and several factors contribute to the difficulty faced by victims. One critical aspect is the power and control dynamics that typify abusive relationships (Elkin, 2018).

Perpetrators often employ manipulative tactics, as seen in the case study, to maintain control over their victims. This can include emotional manipulation, threats, and promises of change (Elkin, 2018). Research by Deitz et al., (2015) emphasizes that victims may be afraid of the consequences of leaving, such as increased violence or harm to themselves or loved ones. The complexity of emotions, including feelings of guilt and attachment, further complicates the decision to leave an abusive relationship.

Another reason is the so-called 'love-bombing' method where the relationship begins as what can be defined to be a perfect status of happiness and love, and from the moment the abuse starts the victim experiences self-blame and tries to adopt strategies to monitor their behaviour in order to avoid abuse and go back to a state of happiness. Delusional hope that 'things can go back to normal' is something that often turns women into prisoners.

When any form of violence occurs in a domestic environment the most common fear in victims is provoking more violence if seeking help, shame, disbelief by others, self-blame and accusations by others, feeling helpless and hopeless, not trusting the criminal justice system and in some occasions a belief that the perpetrator is a good person after all (Markowitz, 2001). All those most common and some less common reasons, prevent the victim from reporting the crime and receiving the crucially important help they need. The offender in most cases uses manipulation and physical force which disables the victim from reacting for typically a long period of time first attempt of getting help (Markowitz, 2001).

Victims of sexual violence are facing many challenges when seeking help. One major barrier is the stigma associated with being a survivor of sexual assault that comes with fear of disbelief, unfair treatment, no trust in the criminal justice system and lack of evidence (Clark, 2007). Stereotypes and myths surrounding sexual assault and rape lead to victim blaming which potentially justifies the perpetrator and provides no support to the victim (Clark, 2007). In cases of alcohol use or a clothing choice is likely to be suggested that the victim provoked the assault which questions the credibility of the victim and suggests they played a role in the assault (Bruke et al., 2020). The attitudes in society can discourage a survivor from seeking help (Hendricks, 2019).

Research has found that rape victims in contrast to victims of other crime, would more often not report the crime (Frese et al., 2004). Not taking action in the case of rape leads the perpetrator to believe that sexual activity without consent is not an act against human rights, it is not punishable and it is not illegal, which furthermore affects heavily the recovery process for the victim (Frese et al., 2004).

Obstruction to healing trauma from sexual assault could cause depression, social anxiety, posttraumatic stress disorder, suicidal intentions, sexually transmitted infections and unwanted pregnancy (Fresco et al. 2011).

Studies found that people assume less offender responsibility if there is clear connection between the victim and the offender, such as a relationship or marriage, in contrast to both not having a relationship, in the case of a stranger rape (Monson et al., 1996). Offenders in acquaintance rape situations are sentenced less in comparison to offenders in stranger rape situations (McCormick et al., 1998).

Rape myth is linked to stereotypical ideas which include 'women cry rape', 'women say no but they enjoy it', 'she asks for it', and 'only the bad girls get raped' (Burt, 1980). The ideology of rape myth is also strongly connected to previous sexual contact, especially in cases of marriage or acquaintance rape, where there might be evidence of previous physical contact, or lack of resistance (Monson et al., 1996).

References

Angelone, D. J., Mitchell, D., & Grossi, L. (2015). Men's perceptions of an acquaintance rape: The role of relationship length, victim resistance, and gender role attitudes. *Journal of Interpersonal Violence, 30*(13), 2278-2303.

Burke, L., O'Higgins, S., Mcivor, C., Dawson, K., O'Donovan, R., & Macneel, P. (2020). The active consent/union of students in Ireland sexual experiences survey 2020: Sexual violence and harassment experiences in a national survey of higher education institutions.

Burt, M. R. (1980). Cultural myths and supports for rape. *Journal of personality and social psychology, 38*(2), 217.

Clark, H. (2007). Judging rape: Public attitudes and sentencing.

Deitz, M. F., Williams, S. L., Rife, S. C., & Cantrell, P. (2015). Examining cultural, social, and self-related aspects of stigma in relation to sexual assault and trauma symptoms. *Violence against women, 21*(5), 598-615.

Elkin, M. (2018). Domestic abuse: findings from the Crime Survey for England and Wales: year ending March 2018. *Office for National Statistics*.

Freccero, J., Harris, L., Carnay, M., & Taylor, C. (2011). Responding to sexual violence: Community approaches. *Sexual Violence & Accountability Project*.

Frese, B., Moya, M., & Megías, J. L. (2004). Social perception of rape: How rape myth acceptance modulates the influence of situational factors. *Journal of interpersonal violence*, *19*(2), 143-161.

Hendricks, A. (2019). Attitudes of Men and Women Toward Sexual Assault: The Role of Stigma, Self-Stigma, and Gender Roles.

https://www.who.int/news-room/fact-sheets/detail/violence-against-women

Markowitz, F. E. (2001). Attitudes and family violence: Linking intergenerational and cultural theories. *Journal of family violence*, *16*, 205-218

McCormick, J. S., Maric, A., Seto, M. C., & Barbaree, H. E. (1998). Relationship to victim predicts sentence length in sexual assault cases. *Journal of Interpersonal Violence*, *13*(3), 413-420.

Monson, C. M., Byrd, G. R., & Langhinrichsen-Rohling, J. (1996). To have and to hold: Perceptions of marital rape. *Journal of Interpersonal Violence*, *11*(3), 410-424.

Samar, S., Khan, U. A., & Razzaq, A. (2023). ATTITUDE AND ACCEPTABILITY TOWARD VICTIMS OF SEXUAL ASSAULT. *Journal of Arts & Social Sciences*, *10*(1), 99-113.

Straton, J. C. (2002). Rule of thumb versus rule of law. *Men and Masculinities*, *5*(1), 103-109.

.